D0417048

Jack the Ripper

The Mystery Solved

Jack the Ripper

THE MYSTERY SOLVED

Paul Harrison

ROBERT HALE · LONDON

First published in Great Britain 1991

ISBN 0 7090 4396 1

Robert Hale Limited
Clerkenwell House
Clerkenwell Green
London EC1R 0HT

Photoset in Palatino by
Derek Doyle & Associates, Mold, Clwyd.
Printed in Great Britain by
St Edmundsbury Press, Bury St Edmunds, Suffolk.
Bound by
WBC Bookbinders Ltd, Bridgend, Glamorgan.

Contents

Illustrations

PICTURE CREDITS

W.H. Allen & Co. Ltd., 1975: 8–9, 19. Crown copyright: 20. All other illustrations photographed by or in the collection of the author.

A book about death and destruction,
yet dedicated with genuine love and affection
to both of my children,
Paula and Mark Harrison

Author's Foreword and Acknowledgements

Never in my wildest dreams did I anticipate completing a book on one of my greatest interests, Jack the Ripper. The research for this book has taken over six years to complete and during this time I have moved home and my two babies have grown into fine children.

The Whitechapel Murders are the archetypal criminal enigma, intriguing all generations who rapidly scan the pages of any new book on the subject, in search of a definitive answer regarding the killer's identity. The greatest problem facing any would-be researcher or author on this series of crimes is the abundant amount of inconsequential data. I would like to feel that this particular work will go a long way in dispelling other theories and tales about the Ripper. This book is based solely upon factual evidence obtained through police circles and official documents in the United Kingdom. As such it does not agree with many, if any, of the previous theories published on the Ripper murders, and it has been possible to prove that many of these are fictional accounts misinterpreted over the last century.

Jack the Ripper has become a permanent resident in my home over the last few years with papers, files and photographs being found in the strangest of places within the house. At one point I had a collection of five knives which had allegedly been handed down through generations as the property of Jack the Ripper. Common sense prevailing, I was forced to store these in my garage until they were eventually given to friends and colleagues who wished to own possible Ripper souvenirs. I myself deemed the knives to be of no real consequence, even if they were authentic they would cause nothing but conjecture and further mystery. It has always amazed me how

Ripperologists proclaim themselves as expert criminologists and detectives. They suddenly become lawyers and jury alike after reading the files on the Whitechapel Murders held at the Public Records Office, Kew, London, regardless of their capabilities as genuine researchers. Few people have been trained in police methods and investigative procedures and the vast majority cannot follow the route of the investigations with any accuracy. Interviews, cross-reference and further cross-reference of available data are the backbone of a good book. Such material is not easily obtained unless one knows where to look and even then it is possible that other criterion prevents the keen researcher from viewing all the relevant information. It is a simple fact of life that other theories have failed to impress the Ripper audience purely because the evidence researched has been weak or misconstrued.

Bearing this point in mind it must be said that no book of this sort could be completed without the assistance of a large number of sources and agencies who were able to locate rare or missing documentation or provide leads as to further research sources. In particular, I would like to thank the following for their assistance: Lesley, for her understanding and support, John and Mary Harrison for their criticism and suggestions, especially when I felt engulfed by the mountainous research data, Chris Wiseman for believing in my instincts and for assisting with the research, the staff of Kettering public library and of Carlisle public library, the staff of the British newspaper at Colindale, Public Records Office at Kew and Chancery Lane, the Greater London Records Office, the Federal Bureau of Investigation (FBI) Quantico, Virginia USA, New Scotland Yard (on countless occasions), the City of London Police, the Metropolitan Police, Northamptonshire Constabulary, *Talk-through* Magazine, the *Criminologist,* Colin Grant and the *Northamptonshire Evening Telegraph,* staff at St Catherine's House, London, and countless staff of public houses within the Whitechapel/Spitalfields district. Special mention also goes to Charlie Bruce who sat and listened to my observations for many hours, Dave Watkins of Radio Northampton who was supportive and influential in the completion of this work, Paul Stevens and Jon Howe for information which they kindly supplied, Ian Griggs who inspired and revealed great enthusiasm in my beliefs and Mr Jack Aspinall, former Chief

Constable of the Ministry of Defence Police who was supportive of my research and allowed me to complete the manuscript without further complications. My appreciation also goes to the thousands of police officers from all over the world, who have supplied information and data which has proved invaluable, and in particular to Chief Inspector Mick Wyatt who proved accurate and helpful in his observations. Finally, I must mention Margaret Willmott who was a source of endless inspiration and without whom much of this work would never have been completed, her belief was unbelievable and proved supportive and influential. I apologize to anyone whom I may have omitted from this list, and ask that they will accept my appreciation.

The monetary values contained within this work are listed in the original pounds, shillings and pence as I believe it maintains fluency and consistency when reading. Certain police reports contain grammatical errors, these have been transcribed as they were originally penned since to alter such evidence would lead to a gross misinterpretation of the facts available.

Any work which has been quoted at length within this book, has to the best of my knowledge been approved by the relevant parties involved, every effort has been made to contact and acknowledge copyright ownership. Should anyone feel aggrieved about being omitted, then please accept this as a genuine mistake and contact me direct so that the situation may be rectified.

1 A World Apart

Any work covering the crimes of Jack the Ripper could not be essayed without first assessing the social and political conditions of Whitechapel and Spitalfields. London in 1888 was very much a tale of two separate worlds. England's capital was in a transitional state expanding and developing every day, and being the largest city in the world her population consisted of many different nationalities and religions. The London most people imagined was that of smart tree-lined garden suburbs with high employment and high wages. In reality, nothing could be further from the truth. The peripheries of the city were well-designed districts, suitable for the wealthy and middle classes. However, the average city-dweller was forced to reside in the inner city areas, some of which were little more than slums. For many of them who ventured to London in search of fame and fortune all that was to be found was filth and deprivation.

Certain London East End locations were classed as the worst areas in the world in which to reside, there were no leafy tree-lined suburbs here, just dozens of dimly lit alleys and courtyards. Whitechapel and Spitalfields were the worst of these areas and the higher social classes tended to ignore and generally avoid contact with the districts. Whitechapel derived its name from the white stone walls of the chapel of ease of St Mary Matfelon, which at one time stood in Whitechapel Road. Dating from the mid-thirteenth century, the chapel was destroyed during the air-raids of 1940 and demolished in 1952, six centuries of history and heritage disappeared without trace. Today, all that remains is a sparse graveyard with the appearance of a small park, in one corner of which stands a fountain with the inscription, 'By one unknown yet well known' – the mystery begins!

Spitalfields lay slightly north of Whitechapel and at one time was the centre of the silk-weaving industry. Today its streets are lined by the large gaunt shells of houses ready for demolition being dangerous as well as eyesores. Walking through the area it soon becomes obvious that at one time it was quite an affluent district, but in 1888 it was devoid of any real employment source, the silk-weaving industry had long since gone, progressing to more pleasant surroundings and working conditions. The large empty houses built by the Huguenots had been transformed into 'Doss' houses, damp dirty hovels which provided a basic shelter for the homeless for a few pennies per night. The population of Whitechapel and Spitalfields consisted of foreigners of whom an estimated thirty per cent were Polish Jews. It was also home to a huge percentage of the criminal slum community, thieves and pick-pockets gathered on every street corner, others lay in the gutters, too drunk or too ill to move. An official report of the time described the scene as follows:

> A noticeable thing in poor streets is the mark left on the exterior of the houses. All along the front about a level of the hips there is a broad mark showing where the men and lads are in constant habit of standing, leaning a bit forward as they smoke their pipes and watch whatever may be going on in the street, while above and below the mortar is picked or kicked from between the bricks.

In every street barefoot children picked what they could from the gutters, other ragged urchins were trained as thieves or pick-pockets. Prison and other records display a direct link between crime and certain social classes. The main criminal offenders of the time seem to have been the Irish cockneys. Their illegal activities would commence at six or seven years old when they would steal into the Victoria Theatre off Whitechapel Road to watch some of the many popular melodramas of the time. It is conceivable that witnessing such scenes of violence and murder led many youngsters to embark upon lives of crime resulting in the more unfortunate criminals being apprehended and finding themselves upon the wrong end of the hangman's rope.

For the majority of the slum community of the East End, relief from this living hell could be found within the many gin palaces and beer houses which were prepared to remain open as long as people were prepared to drink alcohol. Pubs would be full all day and night and in consequence alcoholism was a severe social problem. Overindulgence created a hallucinatory world for the alcoholic to live in, thus eliminating the direct problems of day-to-day life and making a cold night on the street pass much quicker. Mass overcrowding was another problem and it is recorded that in one individual doss-house of nine rooms no less than sixty persons lived and slept. Approximately 8,500 people were without homes and there were an estimated 233 doss-houses for them to sleep in, provided they could find the financial means required to pay for a night. For those with no financial support or assistance it was impossible to find a bed for the night.

Sanitary conditions were best described as despicable, with one toilet (privy) often having to serve up to ten individual households. Privies were also utilized as a sanctuary for the homeless who would cram into the tiny area in an attempt to shelter from inclement weather. Various attempts to reform housing policies were made, but none eased the difficult situation in the East End as the district's immediate problems were not high on the Government's agenda. A local man by the name of the Revd Samuel Augustus Barnett, and his wife Henrietta, resided in Spitalfields, where he preached in St Jude's church in Commercial Street. Independently, Barnett attempted to alleviate the housing problem by creating the East End Dwelling Company which he formed on 1 November 1882. He hoped to demolish the old slums and replace them with larger more fashionable residencies which would house up to three or four families at one time. Although the idea was a good one, it failed to meet the criteria of the homeless who found that when the new buildings were complete they could not afford the rent. Barnett fought furiously with the Authorities, attempting to whip up publicity which could lead to an improvement in facilities, but the Government failed to heed his warnings and continued to improve outer city areas rather than this one district where the human dregs of life resided. By 1888, the whole area had become an aciduous pit of filth and deprivation, poor lighting resulted in a higher number of muggings and assaults and in general the whole district was influential in creating a disaster which was awaiting to happen, it could be claimed that it was the perfect scenario for murder and mystery.

There is an old biblical saying which states 'Man shall not live by bread alone', never was this statement more true than among the people of the East End, many of whom could not afford basic human needs. A stale loaf of bread, perhaps three weeks old, could be purchased from the various street hawkers for around a halfpenny for a four-pound loaf. In some cases this would suffice a small family for almost a week and one cannot imagine what the mouldy bread must have tasted like by the end of the fourth week! Some streets were fortunate enough to have soup kitchens within their boundaries. The homeless would flood into the kitchen in their dozens, each one clamouring for a steaming hot bowl of weak watery soup, and all too often the panic to get to the serving-table caused affrays resulting in street brawls and damage to the soup kitchens and, in consequence, many such kitchens were closed.

It was not only food which was at a premium but good quality water. Some streets were provided with one solitary stand pipe, expected to serve up to sixteen households; it would only provide water for a few minutes each week. Those fortunate enough to be able to afford a piped supply were no better off as they could only rely upon water for approximately nine hours per week. The majority of the water was supplied from the Thames which had been heavily polluted from the overflows of the tanneries and slaughterhouses, its colour was best described as 'Greeny-Black'. In such conditions, human life is forced to survive upon inner strength and courage, as well as the belief that tomorrow will bring a new life and new promises; but for many tomorrow never came, disease riddled the area, typhoid, typhus, rickets were all common and people with stunted physiques thronged the area.

Among the criminal slum community of the district lived hard-working and industrious East-enders, who somehow managed to earn sufficient to provide for their immediate responsibilities. Occasional work was available at Spitalfields or Billingsgate fish market. Others would hawk their wares on the broad northern pavements of the Whitechapel Road, which had the reputation of being one of the city's best markets, where one could purchase anything from a pea right up to a suit of clothes for under a shilling. Slaughterhouses often employed general labourers who would clean and wash down the blood-stained premises. They could often be seen walking down one of the district's main thoroughfares covered in blood, yet no one seemed to notice or care, everyone was too engrossed within their own tiny cocoon of life. In general work was scarce thus requiring people to resort to other more degrading forms of employment. One of the most unsavoury jobs was that of the 'pure finder'. These unfortunate people would scour the streets and alleys in search of fresh dog excrement which would be collected in a bucket and sold to the tanneries for around a shilling per load. 'Pure' being the Victorian euphemism for dog litter. Other people would scavenge the sewers in search of the odd coin or valuable item which might have been dropped down a grate. This was a particularly hazardous task and was generally carried out by the stronger adults of the community; there were regular reports of men going missing or being washed away whilst in the sewers by flash floods, others were quite simply overcome by the sewer rats.

The docks area employed many men and every so often would advertise for a number of male labourers. On one such occasion an employer in this area requested ten strong men to attend for work on the docks. A crowd of over three hundred arrived to claim the jobs, and when the employer opened the gates to his premises to allow the first ten men through an almighty crush ensued, resulting in fights and a near riot situation. Eventually the authorities were called in and quelled the situation, but some thirty men were arrested for their conduct and many others were injured.

Having described a predominantly male world, it must be said that the women and young girls fared no better, with their husbands or companions in jail or constantly absent from home they were forced to fend for themselves. The more fortunate woman gained employment in the tailoring trade, repairing trousers and shirts in one of the dozens of sweat shops which existed. The financial rewards for such work was miserable, but every little helped. Other women worked in match-making factories, though this was not a popular occupation since the factories were often run with strict disciplinary codes, fines were imposed upon the staff for the most trivial breaches of regulations, such as sneezing (1d.) talking (3d.) or swearing (1s.) It came as no real surprise when the match girls went on strike in 1888; their strike was successful with a slight improvement in pay and working conditions.

During the hours of daylight, Spitalfields and Whitechapel were highly industrious areas with an overridingly unpredictable atmosphere, at night-time this atmosphere became hostile and the district was a dangerous location for strangers to pass through. Streets existed which even the hardiest East-ender refused to pass along alone after nightfall, criminals would stand in doorways eagerly watching for the city toff or gentleman in order to attack and rob him. Other streets and alleys were the stomping-ground of literally hundreds of prostitutes who would accost anyone who passed by them. These women were of the lowest possible class, perhaps once they had been fair maidens, but now they had been ravaged by time and ill health and were little more than old hags who had been used and abused. Life upon the streets had been forced upon many of these women by economic stress, others had elected to do it from personal preference. Since many of these women would go for weeks without washing or cleansing themselves, surviving on a diet of stale bread and gin, the aroma which permeated from their bodies and clothing must have been dreadful and it is little wonder that sexual encounters were only brief affairs.

It is difficult to assess the precise number of prostitutes worked in the area, but it is estimated to be around 80,000. There are many problems with this estimate however, for the Victorians described any woman who was kept by a man as a prostitute (hence the saying 'a kept woman'). The most humble of women placed a great deal of emphasis upon their wedding bands and marriage lines as signs of respectability; although, for the average woman, marriage was a pipe-dream and an economic impossibility. The price of a sexual encounter with a Whitechapel prostitute was two pennies, or the cost of a bed in a doss-house for the evening. The sexual act would normally take place outside against a wall or fence as conditions underfoot were not conducive to comfort with pavements and paths being covered in all kinds of excreta and discarded rubbish. This position was further exasperated by the amount of clothing worn by the common prostitute as the client would have to fight his way through layers of vests, petticoats and undergarments before reaching his goal.

Prostitution was a hazardous occupation, not in a violent sense, though this was something which had to be taken into consideration, but in self-preservation. Every so often a smart fresh-faced young prostitute would appear on the streets of the East End, the cause of much grief to older women who would fail to find clients. Therefore an older woman would follow the young prostitute and frighten off would-be clients, until eventually the younger woman would pay her shadow a few pennies to lose herself. As well as the professional prostitutes, there were thousands of amateurs known as 'Dolly Mops', young girls who sexually enticed men for nothing more than fun and adventure often they would end up by becoming professional prostitutes. The law of the street was strict and younger more feeble women would find themselves forced from street to street by the hardier women until there was nothing left but suicide. Bodies were dragged from the Thames regularly and in the majority of cases the corpse was never positively identified.

Victorian society was very much divided with a high percentage of upper and middle classes evident in London, but the lower social scales were far more prominent in the newspapers and their activities were frowned upon by the middle and upper classes. Regular features ran in the pages of the press describing how life was a constant struggle in the East End and the crime reports were eagerly read by those who wished for an insight into life as suffered by the masses. The Victorians in general were enthusiastic readers, especially of newspapers recording dramatic world or local stories. Young boys were employed by many newspapers to sell copies through the streets, and the keen lads would shriek the latest grisly headline as they passed from place to place. Local newspapers employed children of a young age to sell their papers (known as Patterers) which contained the kind of useless information found in today's satirical magazines, none of which was accurate or true. Whether local or national, the press were renowned for their in-depth coverage of morbid subjects, murders were always given full front page coverage as each reporter reasoned why the latest crime had been committed, the public revelled in the sanguinary delights reported with an appetite which was, and still is, seemingly insatiable. The more horrific the report the more copies sold.

With so many agencies reporting crimes, the public could choose which of the many sources of information available it would digest. No two reports on the same crime were identical, although there was a common denominator among all reports – provocative accounts of the ineptitude of the police force. Each newspaper majestically recorded errors made by investigating policemen in a number of cases and if none were apparent then the reporter would ensure that some fictional accounts were added. Unfortunately for the readers of such articles it was difficult to separate fact from fiction and the result was that the public believed all policemen to be incompetent. It was a difficult period for the police force who, in a state of metamorphosis, found themselves discredited by the papers.

Policing an area such as Whitechapel/Spitalfields was at best difficult. The high percentage of habitual offenders living there made crime an everyday occurrence, 'murder' was a not uncommon cry and matters were eased by the fact that the vast majority of victims in murder cases were nameless vagrants. There was a low rate of detection and a high rate of unsolved crimes and murders. Both of these districts were volatile and rebelled against a police presence indeed there were some areas which were decreed as no go areas for single police patrols. Dorset Street, deep in the heart of Spitalfields, was one such area and police patrols preferred to walk its length in pairs. Fleeing criminals often took sanctuary within its boundaries aware that a single officer would not dare to follow.

The City of London was policed by two separate and independent forces, the Metropolitan Police, whose domain was basically the region outside the square mile of the City and the City of London Police whose area covered the square mile. Of the two forces, the Metropolitan Police had undoubtedly the most difficult task, having to encounter criminals residing all over London. It is a recorded fact that few criminals live within the centre of cities since it is easier to pale into insignificance among the masses; apart from that the City, which was for the main staffed by Jews, was a business centre and not suited to ordinary residential or housing policies. The Metropolitan Police were undergoing a great period of change. Sir Edmund Walcott Henderson, an ex-lieutenant-colonel in the Royal Engineers, had taken control of the force in 1868. Aware of the high crime rate he decided to increase the number of detectives in the Criminal Investigations Department (CID), this was a relatively new branch of policing which was still naïve in its knowledge and interpretation of the average criminal and his techniques. Henderson decided that a study of the very efficient French Surête should be carried out in order that the Metropolitan CID could be run along the same lines. The survey was carried out by Howard Vincent who was awarded with the position of Head of CID after he submitted a report of his findings. During his reign at the Metropolitan Police headquarters, Scotland Yard, Vincent became very successful with his management style suiting those who worked beneath him in various staff grades. However, the task was somewhat mundane for Vincent's enthusiastic talents and he resigned, handing over his position to Sir James Monro, an officer of high integrity with a distinguished service record in the Imperial Indian Police where he had been Inspector-General. Sir James's new title with the Metropolitan Force was 'Commissioner CID'.

During the 1880s a large percentage of the CID's work involved the investigation of Fenian (Irish-American) organizations who had been on dynamite missions throughout the United Kingdom. Monro brought into being a special Irish branch of CID to deal with such subversive organizations. Working in close liaison with the Home Office and their political adviser, Doctor Robert Anderson, the Irish branch of the CID attained a good deal of success in countering the various planned attacks by the Fenians and suffocated numerous bombing campaigns. Though it has to be said that the Fenians also had their moments and caused severe embarrassment to the force when they blew up a toilet outside the 'Dynamite Office' at Scotland Yard, shattering many of the windows in the building.

Commissioner Henderson concentrated on his uniformed officers and found that the majority of these were willing men with a will to succeed. It seemed that the problems lay within Scotland Yard rather than with the uniformed branch. In 1886 Henderson made the mistake of allowing the London Workmen's Committee to hold a meeting in Trafalgar Square. On 8 February 1886, thousands of militant and starved men packed the square and eventually rioted, looting shops and destroying property belonging to the middle and upper classes in an open display of rebellion. For almost two hours the whole of the City was in the hands of the mob. Police reinforcements moved in to disperse the rioters, but due to a horrendous act of incompetence a number were directed to Pall Mall to quell the disturbance and others were mistakenly directed to the Mall, only to find it empty. Eventually with the assistance of troops the streets were cleared but at great expense. Many casualties were recorded and damage to businesses was classed as disastrous. There was an immediate cry for Henderson's resignation. Political questions were asked and ultimately Henderson was forced from his seat, resigning after seventeen successful years in the force. The unfortunate Henderson was in fact the first of a number of commissioners who were to fall foul to a cruel twist of fate resulting in the termination of their employment. The fateful day he erred is recorded in the pages of the history books as Black Monday – 8 February 1886. Henderson had undoubtedly provided a solid and secure foundation for the Metropolitan Police to build upon in years to come.

The outgoing commissioner was almost immediately replaced by General Sir Charles Warren KCMG, KCB, RE, FRS. Despite his excellent service record Warren had little idea of police methods and no idea of investigations or how they were carried out. In fact Warren had been given the position through his service career record on which he embarked in 1857 when he joined the Royal Engineers serving in Africa. In 1876 he was appointed Her Majesty's Commissioner to settle the boundaries of the Orange Free State and Griqualand West. He commanded the Diamond Field horse of the Kaffir War in 1878 and was in command of a column and a chief of staff in the Griqua War of 1878–9. In 1882 he moved to Egypt where he was awarded the KCMG, in recognition of his services in bringing to justice the murderers of archaeologist Professor Palmer. He was later made Special Commissioner for Bechuanaland where he successfully protected the Baralongs from the Boers, thus establishing British protectorate in the country – without bloodshed. In 1886 he was awarded with the position as Governor of Suakim and after only a short period in this position he had been summoned to Britain where he was given his latest appointment with the Metropolitan Police.

A keen and devout Christian, Warren was a strict disciplinarian and was not a popular choice for his position among the police or the public. Many words of discontent were uttered in the corridors of power, yet no official complaint was ever recorded against the appointment. Shortly after taking over the helm of Scotland Yard, Warren made a direct enemy of Sir James Monro; at their first meeting, he almost directly told Monro that he was a fool and anything but a gentleman. Warren claimed that all civilians without service experience were idiots and should not be trusted with any responsibility, since the majority of his new force were such civilians and the statement did little to endear Warren to them. Warren instilled military training and discipline into the force with square-bashing taking place every two or three weeks. The new commissioner had agitated and divided the Metropolitan Force and reminded his colleague of his terms of employment, 'I came here to clean up a mess'. Warren could have had no idea of the mess which was to drop well and truly into his lap in the weeks to follow.

Queen Victoria's jubilee year (1887) saw Warren publicly proclaimed as a genius for the way he organized the policing of the capital's traffic congestion problems and crowd control during the celebrations. The higher social classes enjoyed reading of Warren's exploits and approved of his style in dealing with the masses; his opinion of the homeless and the East End was that all such individuals should be given the respect given to a pig in its sty. Sunday 13 November 1887 saw further riots in Trafalgar Square, thousands of the homeless rebelled against Warren and the Government who had displayed little mercy to them in their plight. Many of the homeless were using the square as a sleeping-place and the upper classes condemned the system for allowing them to do so. Warren intervened and decided to evict the vagrants from the square by use of force. Using thousands of police-officers and troops the square was surrounded and the first ever recorded police baton charge took place. The objective was achieved, but at great cost as two civilians were left dead and thousands of others, including women and children were injured. Moreover, any relationship between the police and the public completely disappeared, animosity and contempt festered among the masses. The Trafalgar Square fiasco was known as 'Bloody Sunday' and is one of the most thoughtless operations ever carried out by a British police force. It is without doubt that the police gave as good as they got, but Warren unfairly suppressed the district in an attempt to make himself a popular leader in the eyes of the powers that be.

The press condemned his actions and whipped their readers into a frenzy with accusations of corruptness and mishandling of police matters. Warren had made more enemies than allies and soon found the general public baying for his head and resignation. Warren, though, was a thick-skinned individual and knew that it would take much more than opinion to oust him from his ivory tower; he believed that the judgement of the masses was suspect since in his eyes they lacked any kind of intelligence. Warren remained unsympathetic to the appeals of the press, but as such he had settled his own fate, with serving police-officers turning against him as he continually rejected their claims for increased pension rights (it is a little known fact that he could do little about the matter as the officialdom of red tape shrouded affairs involving pay and rights). Having deflected all the criticism aimed at him after the Bloody Sunday fiasco Warren attempted to run an efficient police force, however, the presence of enemies within his direct ranks meant that he found it difficult to receive information. In 1888 the matters of Scotland Yard were thrust into the public eye when Warren threatened to resign after a difference of opinion with Sir James Monro. The latter proposed that Sir Melville MacNaghton should be elected as assistant head of CID. Initially Warren had agreed with Monro's suggestion, but he altered his opinion when he received information that he was being actively used as a political pawn by Monro. Sir James Monro appealed to the Home Office explaining that Warren had agreed to employ MacNaghton, but at the same time Warren voiced that either he or Monro should resign dependent upon the decision made by the Home Office about MacNaghton. Quite correctly, Warren insisted that he was head of the force and should have overall say and command as to what occurred in the various force departments. Monro resigned and was immediately employed within the Home Office as head of detective service, thus ensuring his contact with the practical running of the CID. Doctor Robert Anderson was elected as his replacement and regularly liaised with Monro without advising Warren that he was doing so. The political wranglings within Scotland Yard were featured in high profile by the press and the affair was portrayed as the fiasco undoubtedly it was. Suddenly the efficient running of a police force had become secondary to the political issues, a precise formula for disaster. The *Pall Mall*

Gazette was astute with its allegations of incompetence among detectives and announced that more than two hundred serious crimes such as rape and murder remained unsolved in the metropolis over a period of just eighteen months, the exact time that Warren had been in office. Suddenly Warren began to feel insecure. Even though the large number of unsolved crimes was not his fault, he was the figurehead of the force whom everyone would blame if things went wrong.

In total contrast to the Metropolitan Police and their problems, the City of London Police appeared to be above reproach, they made good use of the press to portray their image, which was seen as more astute and intelligent than their Metropolitan counterparts. City Commissioner, Sir James Fraser was a likeable sort of character, he had served as chief constable in the Berkshire Constabulary for over nine years and had an exemplary service record prior to this. His direct understudy came in the form of Major Henry Smith, who was later to become acting commissioner. Smith was a native of Scotland and a relative of Robert Louis Stevenson. Before accepting the position with the City Force he had unsuccessfully applied for similar positions in the Northumberland and Liverpool forces. He eventually opted for the position of detective superintendent in the City of London Force fully aware that the assistant commissioner's post was to fall vacant and be offered to him. To his credit he worked hard to understand police methods with enthusiasm and intelligence he was successful on both counts and made studies of every officers' role within the force, the general consensus of opinion among City officers and the public was that the City of London Police was run by two efficient compatible men.

In truth, life within the City force was much more subdued, internal problems being resolved in house rather than being made public scandal. All press releases were studied, scrutinized and checked again before leaving the Old Jewry headquarters. If only Warren had such officers available to him in his office, then perhaps he would have lasted for a much longer term of office and the storm which was brewing on the horizon would not have been so disastrous.

For the people of Whitechapel and Spitalfields the internal wranglings of Scotland Yard and the superiority of their City counterparts were of no consequence. In their mind the police were part of the system which was against them and tended to cause more grief than assistance, especially in their district where men, women and children would hide when they viewed a patrolling policeman – and these were the innocent.

It was a never-ending nightmare that was to crack the foundations of the whole of the City and much of the world. Until then, no one seemed to care and no one intervened with suitable solutions to the everyday problems encountered. Almost like a thunderbolt from hell, one individual challenged the system and defeated it. He drew the attention of the world upon the plight of the East End and its residents. Single-handedly and unintentionally he embarrassed the world's largest police force, mocked surgeons, doctors and government officials alike, as well as terrorizing an entire nation. The mere mention of his name instilled terror into all but the most stupid of people and cleared the streets of children and women alike. Yet this same man was not unusual, he was no weird and wonderful creation, he existed like you and me. He lived a perfectly normal life and was known as a quiet unassuming character to all who knew him. No freemason, no black magician and certainly no different to anyone else – except that he was a man with a deep set need to kill, not indiscriminately but methodically. It is somewhat distressing to know that he was an average person who bore the appearance of an everyday person. He alone knew his real identity. His name was Jack the Ripper!

2 The Unfortunates

Mary Ann Nichols

Bucks Row was in the main a quiet little back street, situated off the Whitechapel Road and running parallel to it. It was an industrial area, its northern side taken up by warehouses and slaughterhouses and a small section of the southern side by tiny terraced houses which were officially classed as cottages. Dominating the skyline at the west end of the street stood the huge London County board school (which still stands to this day). The only illumination provided was a solitary gas lamp which situated opposite the board school, at night it became a particularly suspect area due to the distinct lack of lighting.

At 3.40 a.m. Friday 31 August 1888, Charles Cross turned into Bucks Row from its eastern entrance off Brady Street. Cross was on his way to work at Pickfords in the City Road. As he increased his pace along the dark street he saw what he initially thought was a tarpaulin lying in the gateway of a stableyard near the board school. Believing that it might be something of value he crossed the road to approach it; to his surprise he found it was the body of a woman. His initial reaction was that she was too drunk to stand but he then noticed that her dress had been pulled up around her midriff. Fearing that she might have been the victim of a sex attack he was about to revive her when he suddenly heard footsteps approaching from behind him. In a panic Cross hid in the shadows for he feared that it might be the attacker returning. As the individual approached, Cross realized that it was someone on their way to work. Stepping out from the shadows, he exclaimed, 'Come and look over here, there's a woman'. The other man, whose name was John Paul, approached the body, stooping down and looking directly into her face. Cross took hold of the woman's hands which felt slightly warm, and murmured, 'I think she is dead.' He then felt the unfortunate female's face which like her hands was slightly warm.

Paul placed his head upon the woman's breast to try to find any trace of a heart-beat. He believed he had and said, 'I think she is still breathing, but it is very little if she is.' In a vain attempt to maintain the woman's decency, Paul attempted to pull the woman's dress down over her knees, but could not move it. Both men left the body in search of a police-officer.

A few minutes later they met Constable 55H Mizen in Bakers Row. Cross informed him, 'There's a woman lying in Bucks Row, she is either dead or drunk.'

At this point Paul added, 'I think she is dead.' Constable Mizen accepted the men's claim and hurried to the scene which had by this time been discovered by another patrolling police-officer.

Constable 97J John Neil entered Bucks Row at 3.45 a.m. with little on his mind but where he could call into next for a warm from the damp night air. On passing the board school he found the body and, as he shone his bull's-eye lantern upon the form below him, he became aware of the severity of the attack; blood oozed from a great gash in the woman's neck. Constable Neil flashed his lantern in the direction of Brady Street where he knew his colleague Constable 96J Thain was on patrol. Thain returned the signal and rushed to Neil's assistance. Once there, he was instructed to bring Doctor Llewellyn from 152 Whitechapel Road. In the meantime, Constable Mizen ran for an ambulance. While all this was being done Neil noted the position of the body and injuries, he later stated, 'The female's eyes were wide open, she was laying on her back with her head facing eastwards. The body was still quite warm, the left arm straight and touching the gates to the stableyard.' Beside the body, a black bonnet which lay upon the cold damp cobbles. Blood from the gash in the woman's neck had run into the gutter and surrounding paved area. At this time no one realized that a crime of any notoriety had taken place. It seemed a typical murder similar to others committed in that district over a period of years.

At 4.00 a.m. Doctor Ralph Llewellyn arrived. Parting his way through a small crowd of spectators who had gathered round the body, the doctor made a cursory examination of the body using the light of the police constables' bull's-eye lanterns. He duly pronounced life extinct and instructed that the body be removed to the mortuary in Old Montague Street.

Subsequent enquiries in Bucks Row revealed that no one had heard or seen anything suspicious. Mrs Emma Green lived next to the murder site and Walter Purkess lived opposite. Both had spent a sleepless night, yet neither had heard any sound. It was a similar story elsewhere in Bucks Row, and it appeared that the murder had been committed in total silence with no witnesses.

On arrival at the mortuary, the dead woman's body was not touched by either of the two paupers until they had eaten their breakfast. Eventually the clothes were removed from the body in order that the skin could be washed down. Inspector Helson of J division was detailed to attend the mortuary in order to itemize the woman's possessions and to ascertain her identity. To his horror, the inspector found on his arrival at the mortuary that the female's clothing had been removed and thrown into a corner. In addition, the body which he viewed upon the slab was not the simple murder case which he had been requested to handle. According to the information he had received, the woman in Bucks Row had sustained injuries to her neck only. The woman upon the slab had such injuries but she had also been disembowelled. Surely such a fact could not have gone unnoticed?

Helson demanded that Doctor Llewellyn attend the mortuary immediately to confirm that it was the same body. Llewellyn attended and admitted that he had missed the mutilations during his earlier examination. The astute inspector alerted Scotland Yard of the new information and requested further assistance, which arrived in the form of Inspector Spratling. Together both officers worded a report regarding the injuries received by the dead woman. The report stated:

> Her throat had been cut from left to right, two distinct cuts being on the left side, the windpipe, gullet and spinal cord being cut through, a bruise apparently of a thumb being on the right lower jaw, also one on left cheek. The abdomen had been cut open from centre of bottom of ribs, on the right side and under pelvis to the left of the stomach, there the wound was jagged. The omentium, or coating of the stomach was also cut in several places and there were some small stabs on private parts, apparently done with a

> strong bladed knife, supposed to have been done by some left-handed person, death almost instantaneous.

The only clue the police had was the fact that the killer might well be left-handed. Many officers believed it to be another gang murder, others hoped as much since it had been an awfully long time since such a murder of this kind had been committed in London. The thought that a lone operator might commit such atrocities was a worrying one, especially since the *modus operandi* was not evident. Gang murders tended to be more horrific; and gangs would often murder common whores to frighten other women into paying their pimps who usually belonged to gangs.

A description of the dead woman was circulated to all local police stations in the hope that someone would recognize her:

> aged about forty five years, being five foot two or three inches, dark brown hair turning grey, brown eyes. Wearing a brown ulster with several brass buttons attached (figure of a female riding a horse and a man at the side thereon), brown linsey frock, grey woollen petticoat, flannels, brown stays, black ribbed woollen stockings, men's side spring boots which were cut on the uppers and both of which had tips on the heels, and finally a black straw bonnet trimmed with black velvet.

The only clue as to the identity of the woman was stamped upon the lining of the flannel undergarments she had been wearing. The words 'Lambeth Workhouse PR' were clearly visible showing them to be the property of the Lambeth Workhouse in Princes Road. Police attended the workhouse and spoke to numerous occupants. A young woman known as Mary Ann Monk volunteered to view the body and on doing so claimed it was that of Polly Nichols whom she had last seen some seven weeks earlier in a public house in New Kent Road. Both had been residents of the Lambeth Workhouse. Apart from that, little else was gained from the people who attended the workhouse. Most people refused to become involved in such incidents since there was a common belief that to interfere could well mean that the unsuspecting volunteer quickly became a suspect. Despite this, the police attempted to piece together as much information on the dead woman as they could. Edward Walker of Camberwell also attended the mortuary and confirmed the body to be that of his daughter Mary Ann (Polly) Nichols.

Polly Nichols was born on 26 August 1845 in Shoe Lane, London. Her maiden name was Walker. On 16 January 1864, she married printer's machinist William Nichols and the couple lived in a doss-house in Bouverie Street. They had five children. But Polly Nichols was not up to the permanent responsibilities of a family and often drifted from her home wandering through the streets in a drunken stupor and, one suspects, soliciting. The marriage ended in 1880 when Polly claimed that her husband had run off with the midwife following the birth of their fifth child. In reply, William Nichols told friends that their marriage had in fact ended because of his wife's dependence on alcohol. Whatever her reasons, Polly abandoned the family home in search of more suitable surroundings, and quickly entered into another relationship with a man called Thomas Stuart Drew. However, due to her lack of loyalty this relationship was terminated rather abruptly, and from here Polly drifted into a life of abuse and vagrancy. Workhouse records show that she resided at many such establishments including Lambeth, St Giles, Edmonton and Mitcham.

There was a brief respite in April 1888 when she found employment as a maid with the Cowdry household at Ingleside, Rosehill Road, Wandsworth. The family were of a strict religious background and as such were completely teetotal. Polly found life without her blessed alcohol very difficult. It came as no surprise when after six weeks she absconded with £3.10s. worth of clothing. From here Polly moved to Whitechapel/Spitalfields where she regularly resided in doss-houses in Dorset Street, Thrawl Street and Flower and Dean Street (known locally as Flowery Dean). No. 56 Flower and Dean Street was her last known address.

Mary Ann Nichols was a quiet woman who generally kept herself to herself. She led an apparently normal lifestyle and had been given every opportunity to better herself which she failed to accept. It would seem that it was this abhorrent dislike of responsibility that was the cause of her downfall. After many months tramping the streets of the East End, Polly had become quite a resilient character. It proved a suitable life for the poor woman as she drifted from one crisis to another with little care as to the outcome. Yet Polly was living in her own private nightmare, she had become lost within the system with no hope of return nor of any real future. It suited her to remain anonymous among the masses, but unknown to her she was to become one of the most well-known persons in Britain. The name Polly Nichols was to become synonymous with that of the famous Jack the Ripper.

The police eventually obtained sufficient information to piece together the final few hours of Polly Nichols' life.

Friday 31 August 1888 was just another day in the life of Polly Nichols. Having spent most of the previous night hawking her body and wasting the meagre sum earned on her beloved alcohol, Polly found to her surprise that she had a few pennies available to buy the black bonnet she wanted and eagerly visited the shop and paid her deposit. This done, Polly resumed her slow patient walk of the streets and back alleys of the district searching for would-be customers. Soon the chill of the cool autumn air began to chill her, her well-worn clothes could no longer maintain the body heat she so desperately needed. Reaching into her pocket, Polly searched for the four pennies required for a bed. The search was of no avail, once again she was broke. Instinctively she made her way to 18 Thrawl Street, one of her favourite dosses. Once there sat herself by the stove in the kitchen and soaked in as much heat as was humanly possible. At 1.40 a.m., the doss-house deputy entered the kitchen and requested fourpence for a bed. Polly replied, 'Will you save a bed for me, I'll soon get my doss money, see what a jolly bonnet I've got now.' It was a pathetic gesture, for Polly knew that she would find it difficult to find a customer at that time of morning. The comment about her bonnet reveals the false hope in her mind that the bonnet enhanced her appearance and might attract more clients. The next fifty minutes of her life are missing, but it is likely that she went in search of further customers wandering the streets and visited various pubs on the way.

At 2.30 a.m. Emily Holland, a personal friend of Polly's, was crossing the Whitechapel Road *en route* to 18 Thrawl Street when she saw Polly staggering down Osborn Street towards her. The women stopped to talk and Polly explained her plight, bragging that she had spent all of her earnings on drink, she also stated that she was going in search of another client to earn her doss money. Emily Holland quickly realized that Polly was in no fit state to venture out into the night and asked her to return to Thrawl Street with her, Polly refused and danced off in an easterly direction along Whitechapel Road. This is the last official sighting of Polly Nichols who, some seventy minutes later, was to become the first official victim of Jack the Ripper …

The inquest into her death opened on Saturday 1 September 1888 at the Working Lads Institute on Whitechapel Road. The presiding coroner was Mr Wynne Edwin Baxter, an ex-lawyer of some considerable standing. Baxter had been the official coroner for two years and he had a deep-rooted dislike of the police. The room designated for the inquest was filled to capacity for the murder had attracted the attention of a whole community who eagerly awaited the full gory details of the crime. Various witnesses were called to give evidence and much inconsequential data was heard. Police-officer John Neil, who was the first official to view the body, explained that he had walked along Bucks Row some thirty minutes before he found the body and it was then clear. No evidence was heard in relation to the description of the killer and, at the request of the police, Baxter adjourned the hearing until Monday 3 September 1888. It was later moved to 17 September 1888 since the police had failed to find any further information.

The police intended to use the opportunity of a delay in the hearing by ascertaining further evidence which would create a more professional image of themselves. However, by a cruel twist of fate, all of their intentions were ruined when, on the morning of Saturday 8 September, a second woman was found butchered in the rear yard of 29 Hanbury Street. It was confirmed that the killer was also Polly Nichols' slayer.

The inquest into Polly Nichols' death resumed on 17 September and once again Baxter appeared to derive some pleasure from chastising the police for their apparent ineptitude in failing to find any further evidence. Once again, he adjourned the hearing until 22 September, advising the jury that he would require a verdict on that day. Yet again, the police had no further information so Baxter commenced his summing-up of the case. To everyone's surprise he referred to two other cases of murder which had occurred in the district, those of Emma Smith and of Martha Tabram. Emma Smith was a 45-year-old prostitute who had been violently attacked on Monday 3 April 1888 by a gang of youths in Osborn Street, she had been raped and a large blunt stick had been thrust into her vagina tearing the perineum. Smith eventually died of her injuries, but before doing so she gave a description of her assailants to the police. Martha Tabram (Turner) was thirty-nine years of age and also a prostitute. She had been found brutally murdered in George Yard Buildings in the early hours of Tuesday 7 August 1888. Her body had received thirty-nine separate stab wounds, almost every major organ had been punctured by a long-bladed knife.

Coroner Baxter declared that in his opinion these murders were both connected with the death of Polly Nichols. The official reaction from the police was disbelief. They denied Baxter's suggestions and claimed that Emma Smith had been murdered by one of the local 'High Rip' gangs, and that Tabram was killed by an unknown assailant. The latter crime they saw as being similar to dozens of others over a period of twenty or so years – certainly they did not feel it was linked to the Bucks Row murder.

The press seized the opportunity to link numerous crimes with the recent tragedies in the Whitechapel district. Some newspapers actually implied that the killer was some kind of super-being in the form of a beast, half-man, half-animal. The initial hounding of the police was beginning to gain momentum, and a whole nation asked the same questions. Why had the police not yet gained any description of the killer? Why had they no apparent interest in the incidents, but treated them with contempt? Of course no police force would dare to do either of the latter insinuations. The simple facts of the matter were that the authorities had not one clue available to them, the killer was of a very devious nature and would not be caught easily. Yet they could not announce such information as it would cause widespread panic.

Polly Nichols was buried on Thursday 6 September 1888 at Ilford cemetery. A number of people were present along with her ex-husband William and three of her children. It is reported that when William Nichols viewed the body of his late wife on the slab at the mortuary he had commented, 'I forgive you as you are now, for what you have done to me.' At the graveside he made no comments other than to comfort his younger children. It was a more graceful end to the couple's relationship than she deserved. Polly Nichols had no further problems, yet even in death she created problems for others.

For the people of Whitechapel, Jack the Ripper had commenced his roll call.

Eliza Ann Chapman

Hanbury Street runs east to west through the heart of Spitalfields. A narrow street, in 1888 it was lined by typical Victorian houses, many of which had been converted into shops or doss-houses. It was quite an average street, but was then classed as a better part of the district. No. 29 Hanbury Street was owned by Mrs Amelia Richardson who made a decent living from letting out rooms within her house.

At 4.45 a.m. Saturday 8 September 1888, Amelia's son John Richardson called at 29 Hanbury Street in order to check the doors of the rear cellar which had recently been damaged by would-be burglars. The cellar doors were situated in the rear yard of the house, access to which was gained by a side door at the front of the house which led down a passage of some thirty-odd feet in length through the house. At the end of the passage, three stone steps led down into the compressed earth yard. John Richardson sat on the top step of the yard in order to trim some leather from his boots which were pinching him. On completing this task he stepped down into the yard, checked the cellar doors which were secure and left the house via the same route.

It was 5.45 a.m. the same morning when John Davis, a resident of the house, awoke from his slumbers and prepared himself for work. Sunlight made an attempt to shine through the dark grubby windows of the house and as he looked out of the window he saw that it was a cold dry morning. He could hardly have felt too happy since his night's rest had been continually disturbed by his children who had been playing up all night. Davis left his first-floor room and descended the stairs which led into the side passage of the house. As usual, the front entrance door was wide open. Begrudgingly, Davis walked along the passage to the tap in the rear yard in order to throw some cold water over his face. As he pulled the rear yard door open, he saw the blood-covered body of a woman lying on her back to the left of the three stone steps. Davis was momentarily stunned by the scene, but once it began to penetrate his brain he fled in terror, running back along the passage and out onto Hanbury Street, Davis met two men from Bayleys, a firm of packing-case makers in the street and informed them of his find and both men rushed to the scene. The severity of the mutilations made it instantly obvious that the woman was dead, so both men ran to Commercial Street police station where they reported the facts to Inspector John Chandler of H division. Instantly, Chandler detailed a number of officers to attend the scene to clear the street. On his arrival at Hanbury Street a few minutes later, Chandler found the rear yard containing the body full of people who were clamouring to see the body. He at once instructed his constables to clear the yard and house and to stand guard at both doors preventing any curiosity-seekers from removing or touching vital evidence which might be available. In reality, it might have been too late for such action, as unknown items could have been removed prior to his arrival. A constable was sent to 2 Spital Square, the home of the divisional surgeon doctor George Bagster Phillips. While waiting for the doctor to arrive, Chandler noted in his official report:

> In the back yard found a woman lying on her back, dead, left arm resting on left breast, legs drawn up. Abducted small intestines and flap of abdomen lying on right side above right shoulder attached by a cord with the rest of the intestines inside the body. Two flaps of skin from the lower part of the abdomen lying in a large quantity of blood above left shoulder, throat cut deeply from left and back in a jagged manner right around throat.

Doctor Phillips arrived at 6.30 a.m. and immediately pronounced life extinct. He instructed that the body should at once be removed to a local mortuary. By sheer coincidence the body was transported in exactly the same casket as that which had removed the remains of Polly Nichols eight days before.

With the body removed, the police inspector and the doctor commenced a detailed search of the yard in an attempt to find a clue or incriminating evidence. This was quite a task as the yard measured some fifteen feet by twelve feet and was surrounded by an old wooden fence. Where the body had lain, the officials found a piece of muslin, a comb and two pieces of paper, all of which appeared to have fallen from the dead woman's pockets either during or after the attack. Where her feet had lain, two brass rings and two new farthings were found, these appeared to have been placed there rather than fallen. In view of the number of people who had already been in the yard, the inspector immediately ruled out any ulterior motive behind this fact. In his opinion anyone could have placed the articles there. Close examination of the items found revealed that one of the pieces of paper bore the insignia of the Sussex Regiment along with the letter M and a postmark (London 28 Aug. 1888). The inspector at once realized that this could be a vital clue and retained the paper which subsequently transpired to be the corner of an envelope. Beneath the water tap in the yard a wet leather apron was found. Quite naturally, Chandler felt pleased with himself and declared that it was only a matter of time before the killer was caught. He said that the perpetrator of the crime had left a number of clues which would be easily followed up. In the mean time, Chandler's immediate problem was to identify the dead woman.

The murder scene became so popular with sightseers that local residents charged them for a view of the yard from their house windows.

News of the latest slaughter quickly spread around the area and a full description of the dead woman was circulated to all local forces and stations, resulting in an early confirmation of the woman's identity. Timothy Donovan, the deputy house-keeper at Crossinghams Lodgings, 35 Dorset Street, attended the mortuary and viewed the body which he declared to be that of Eliza Ann Chapman (Dark Annie).

Born in 1841, Eliza Ann Smith had been brought up in and around London. Her father was a private in the 2nd Battalion of Lifeguards. On 1 May 1869 she married a coachman named John Chapman and for a short time the couple lived in Bayswater before moving to the very respectable area of Windsor where John Chapman gained employment as the head domestic coachman to a farm bailiff, Josiah Weeks. The couple had three children, one boy and two girls, and appeared to lead an idyllic life. But all was not what it seemed, for Mrs Chapman enjoyed the company of other men and had a strong desire for alcohol. It was not long before she earned herself a rather promiscuous reputation which was brought to her husband's attention. This led to many violent confrontations during which Annie was prone to throwing anything within her grasp at her better half. By 1882, John Chapman had taken as much as he could suffer and ended the marriage. Annie left Windsor for the more depressing climate of Whitechapel. Shortly after her departure one of her daughters died. John Chapman foolishly agreed to pay Annie an allowance of ten shillings per week thus ensuring that she had sufficient financial aid to keep a roof over her head. In 1886 the allowance ceased and Annie, who had by now become an established prostitute, made enquiries as to why her husband had failed to meet his responsibilities. To her surprise she found that he was dead and, although she was unaware of the fact at the time, this was the final straw in her life and she soon became destitute.

Like the majority of her profession at that time, Annie soon lost all sense of values. She had no self-respect and would live one day at a time with the arrival of each morning bringing a new crisis and fresh problems. Her one goal each day was to earn sufficient money from whoring to find a bed that evening; health was secondary to this fact. Annie Chapman became very ill, suffering from tuberculosis.

On Monday 3 September 1888, Amelia Farmer saw Annie in Dorset Street. Feeling concerned about her bedraggled appearance, she asked her what her problem was. Annie explained that she felt unwell and displayed various bruises about her body which matched the one above her right eye, these had been sustained during a fight with a fellow prostitute over a bar of soap and a man. After receiving assurances from Annie Chapman about the state of her health, Amelia Farmer resumed her normal business. The following day she again met Chapman, this time near Spitalfields church. Chapman was highly distressed and informed her friend that she had not had so much as a cup of tea that day. Farmer provided her with money to purchase tea and told her not to spend it on rum or alcohol. Annie agreed and informed Farmer that it was her intention to go to the casual ward for treatment. Amelia Farmer last saw Annie Chapman at 5.00 p.m. on Friday 7 September 1888 in Dorset Street. When the concerned friend had asked Annie why she had not gone to the casual ward as she had intended, Annie told her that she felt too ill to do anything and added, 'It's no use my giving way, I must pull myself together or I shall have no lodgings.'

The last days or hours of any murder victim's life are usually difficult to trace, but the police investigating the death of Annie Chapman were successful in the extreme and ascertained her precise actions for her last forty-eight hours on this earth. On the afternoon preceding her death Annie remained in the kitchen of 35 Dorset Street. At this time she had money as she was also sighted in the Ten Bells public house in Commercial Street and later in Ringers Bar, Dorset Street. At 1.45 a.m., on the morning of her death, Timothy Donovan had approached her as she sat warming herself in the kitchen of 35 Dorset Street and requested the money for a bed. Annie told Donovan that she had no money, but would go out and find some, requesting that he keep her bed for her as she always slept in bed No. 29. Tired and somewhat dejected, Annie Chapman rose to her feet and shuffled out of the warm kitchen into the cold dark streets of Whitechapel. John Evans, the nightwatchman from the same premises, saw Annie shuffle down Dorset Street via Paternoster Row and out into Brushfield Street. She was, he claimed, slightly intoxicated but not drunk. It is obvious that she encountered some difficulty in finding another customer that morning as she never returned to the lodging-house. Her next customer was in all probability her last.

Elizabeth Long passed through Hanbury Street at around 5.30 a.m. There she claimed to have seen a woman who fitted Chapman's description talking to a man, whom she described as aged over forty with a shabby-genteel appearance. He had the look of a foreigner and was wearing a dark coat and a deerstalker hat. The couple were standing outside 29 Hanbury Street and as Mrs Long passed them she overheard the man say, 'Will you?', and the woman reply, 'Yes'. If this information is correct, then the man with Annie Chapman was her eventual killer and he had almost thirty minutes to complete his task in broad daylight. What cannot be regarded as accurate is Long's estimation of the age of the man. Life was not easy in Whitechapel and Spitalfields and like the prostitutes men would become prematurely aged. It is also unclear why she felt that the man had the appearance of a foreigner?

The police foolishly informed the press that a direct clue as to the identity of the killer had been found in the rear yard of Hanbury Street in the form of a leather apron. Immediately the press printed this information, emblazoning it across the pages of their newspapers, and created a most disturbing incident for an innocent man. Eager reporters explained that local people had informed them of a man known as 'Leather Apron' who was in the habit of threatening prostitutes. At once 'Leather Apron' was presumed guilty without fair hearing. On Monday 10 September 1888, Detective Sergeant John Thicke called at 22 Mulberry Street and arrested a bootmaker known as John Pizer who was also known as 'Leather Apron'. A search of Pizer's home was carried out and resulted in the police seizing a number of sharp knives and some women's hats. These were immediately linked with Polly Nichols who spoke of her new bonnet on the night of her death. Pizer was taken to Leman Street police station where he admitted being in hiding as his brother-in-law had advised him that he was being branded locally as the killer. He had therefore hidden at 22 Mulberry Street the four days before his arrest. This was confirmed by members of his family, but a number of discrepancies still existed which Pizer had to answer. The police obviously suspected Pizer and questioned him concerning his whereabouts on the night of Polly Nichols' death. Pizer revealed that he had stayed at Crossmans Lodgings in the Holloway Road. He had spoken to a police constable there just as the church clock was striking. Pizer claimed that he had asked the officer about a fire which was raging on the Ratcliff dry dock and they spoke about the fire before Pizer bid the officer a goodnight. The police-officer concerned was questioned and confirmed the story was correct. The police had arrested an innocent man. This fact was quickly released to an impatient press who failed to agree with police conclusions. For reasons of safety, Pizer remained in police custody until the hue and cry had died down and he was officially declared innocent. The ordeal of the 33-year-old Jewish bootmaker was over. Interestingly, a contemporary sketch of Pizer was published in the *Daily Telegraph*. In it, Pizer is depicted as a Fagin-style character looking like a criminal.

Monday 10 September 1888 was also the first day of the inquest into the death of Eliza Ann Chapman. Once again the venue was the Alexandria Rooms of the Working Lads Institute in Whitechapel Road and Coroner Baxter was given the dubious honour of being the presiding officer with Mr Collier acting as his assistant. The jury viewed the final remains of Annie Chapman, then returned to the hearing where one by one the various witnesses were called to reveal the life led by Annie Chapman. Albert Cadoche a 31-year-old carpenter of 31 Hanbury Street told of how at approximately 5.20 a.m. on the morning of 8 September he had been in the rear yard of 31 Hanbury Street when he heard what he thought was a woman saying 'No'. He then heard a noise which would have been conducive with a body slumping against a fence. This evidence was in direct contradiction of that given by Elizabeth Long, but various factors must be taken into consideration before one makes a categorical statement about the conflicting details given at the inquest. Firstly, how did Cadoche know what the sound of someone falling against a fence would be like, and secondly, why was he not more inquisitive about it especially after he heard a woman cry 'No' twice? It goes without saying that the evidence that Annie Chapman was in the rear yard of a house in Hanbury Street, leads us to conclude that she was with a male companion for what she thought was sex, but what he wanted was murder.

One cannot assume anything in murder cases. Many commentators on these crimes believe that witnesses were quite incorrect about the precise times when they believe they saw or heard something. My personal experience contradicts this. I and many of my colleagues have always found that witness testimony is normally very accurate, especially with regard to time. However, witnesses often infer that events relate to particular crimes or individuals. In the case of Annie Chapman, we must conclude that Elizabeth Long could have seen any courting couple, but for Cadoche to have heard sounds coming from the yard where the murder was committed is too much of a coincidence. Therefore I tend to believe Cadoche and his timing of the event.

The inquest was adjourned after lengthy questioning of the various witnesses and when it resumed on 12 September one of the first witnesses called was John Pizer who explained his various alibis for the nights in question. He also explained that the long-bladed knives were tools of his trade, the women's hats were a little side-line he had just started selling. John Pizer was completely exonerated from the enquiries and expelled from the inquest and further police and public harassment. He was later to sue many leading newspapers successfully for libel damages. Once more the police suffered from the criticisms of Baxter and the public. It soon became evident that they had at times been somewhat inefficient. No plan, map or sketch of the rear yard in Hanbury Street had been submitted for official reference purposes. Mr Baxter made a great deal of this fact and ensured that the public were aware of his personal feelings on the matter.

Despite the verbal barrage at the inquest the police continued to make steady progress with their enquiries. The piece of envelope found near the body of Annie Chapman bearing the insignia of the Sussex Regiment proved to be a false alarm. Inspector Chandler had been detailed to make enquiries at the regiment's headquarters at Farnborough. Chandler returned from his enquiries with the sad news that the piece of envelope found could have been purchased by anyone living in the Farnborough region. Despite all efforts, no direct links could be made between anyone serving in the regiment and Whitechapel. Once again valuable time and energy had been expended on apparently pointless enquiries, yet every avenue had to be covered.

Meanwhile at Scotland Yard Inspector Frederick Abberline was the latest addition to the squad in search of the Whitechapel killer.

The police continued to probe but were on a hiding to nothing with no direct clues available and not one individual witness who had unquestionably seen the killer or the victim. There was little they could do but sit and wait for another attack. Further arrests were made, but almost every individual could provide a suitable alibi for their movements on the nights concerned. A particularly high percentage of criminal lunatics were arrested and incarcerated in mental asylums. By now the police were prepared to listen to anyone who offered the least likely suspect. Inspector Abberline personally arrested Walter Henry Piggott in the Pope's Head public house, who had entered the pub and bragged to all and sundry that he was the killer. Abberline questioned his latest suspect at Commercial Street police station. Visually Piggott displayed all the attributes one would expect of a killer, he was covered in blood and had bite marks on his hands, yet he provided suitable explanations for these marks and the blood. Once again it seemed the police were barking up the wrong tree. Abberline assessed Piggott as a glory-seeker mentally obsessed about the crimes; to ensure that he could not commit copy-cat murders, Abberline had Piggott certified insane and incarcerated in a lunatic asylum.

Inspector Chandler was still plugging away with enquiries into Annie Chapman's death and he submitted the following report which finally confirmed the mystery of the envelope piece found in the rear yard of 29 Hanbury Street:

> I beg to add that at 11 a.m. 15th inst, William Stevens a painter of 35 Dorset Street, Spitalfields, Common Lodging house, came to Commercial Street police station and made the following statement. I know Annie Chapman as a lodger in the same house, I know that on Friday 7th inst the day before the murder, she came into the lodging house and said she had been to the hospital, and intended going to the infirmary the next day, I saw that she had a bottle of medicine, a bottle of lotion and a box with two pills in, and as she was handling the box it came to pieces, she then took out the two pills and picked up a piece of paper from the kitchen floor near the fireplace, and wrapped the pills up in it. I believe the piece of paper with Sussex regiment thereon to be the same. I do not know of any lodger in the house who has been in the army.

Chandler goes on, 'I beg to add that 35 Dorset Street is a common lodging house and frequented by a great many strangers, and it is very probable it may have been dropped by one of them.'

With no such thing as forensic science to assist them, the police were doing an excellent job in solving minor discrepancies. From the report submitted by Chandler, it can be seen that the police were very efficient in their enquiries – all that they lacked was that vital clue which would afford them a breakthrough.

By the time of his summing-up on 26 September 1888, Baxter had opened and adjourned the Chapman inquest on no less than three occasions. Baxter explained the medical evidence suggested the victim's uterus had been removed by the killer for a special purpose. He continued:

> The organ had been taken by one who knew where to find it, what difficulties he would have to contend against and how he should use his knife so as to abstract the organ without injury to it. No unskilled person could have known where to find it, or have recognized it when found. For instance, no mere slaughterer of animals could have carried out this operation, it must have been someone accustomed to the post-mortem room.

This was supposition. Baxter should have known better than to speculate on the profession of the killer when no definite facts were available. As a result, a bewildered police force was now inundated with claims that the killer must be a mad doctor or surgeon with a vendetta against prostitutes. Baxter had obviously noted a comment made during the inquest by Doctor Phillips who stated, 'Obviously the work was that of an expert or one at least who had such knowledge of anatomical or pathological examinations, as to be enabled to secure the pelvic organs, with one sweep of the knife.' Once again we are met by an inference. The claim that the organs were removed by one sweep of the knife is ridiculous. Phillips should have stated that before the uterus was removed other organs had to be removed and these had been hacked about. Any organs missing had been removed by a clumsy hand. Phillips also commented on the murder weapon, 'It could well be a post-mortem knife or a well ground slaughterman's knife, with a blade of five to six inches.' There can be no question about the doctor's qualification to make such a definite statement regarding the style and type of murder weapon, and he does not attempt to name the killer's profession. Baxter's reckless statement was of no real assistance to anyone concerned with the enquiry. Baxter waffled on for hours and it came as no surprise when the jury returned a verdict of wilful murder by person or persons unknown.

Once more the media began to speculate about the killer's identity. They reached the ridiculous conclusion that the killer was a ghostly spectre who haunted the back streets and alleyways of Whitechapel and was invisible to patrolling police-officers. The press also aided the killer by pointing the accusing finger at different social classes.

The credibility of a police force has never before been jeopardized in such a manner; the morale of the subordinate officers had reached its lowest ever level. Many of the officers on the ground would procure information which they felt was vital to the enquiry, yet they found their evidence was either ignored or misconstrued and lost within the system. As varying amounts of pressure were applied to senior police officials by the Home Office and the public, the upper echelons of the police force began to ignore the comments being made by the officers who were carrying out the basic investigations. As the police lost confidence, the press gained total control of the police operation and used this to their full advantage. The crimes of the Whitechapel murderer had now become the basis of a personal vendetta between high-powered officials and a solitary individual who was successfully destroying their reputations.

The prostitute killer had begun to enjoy his new-found notoriety. He was nobody's fool and quickly recognized that the police were being misguided by official sources and the media. Taking a totally reckless attitude, he elected to taunt the police and the authorities and at the same time christen himself. He chose a name most appropriate to his style of work – the name of Jack the Ripper.

Meanwhile Annie Chapman was buried on Friday 14 September 1888 at Manor Park cemetery. It was a quiet funeral with only a few close relatives in attendance. Annie Chapman slipped quietly from this world in much the same way as she had led her life with little fuss.

Dear Boss

The mass public condemnation of the police meant there was little surprise when members of the public decided to take the law into their own hands in an attempt to outsmart the foolish detectives and to catch the killer red-handed. One such group formed for this purpose was the Whitechapel Vigilance Committee headed by George Lusk, a local well-to-do businessman. This group was formed on 10 September 1888 in response to dwindling business in the district due to the killer's activities. George Lusk, like almost everyone else, had become disillusioned by the media reports, and one suspects that his attempts to rid the streets of this terror were genuine.

The Vigilance Committee were an enthusiastic lot, full of good intentions which were well publicized by the press, they promised a substantial reward for information leading to the arrest, yet despite all this they failed to capture the public's imagination. The substantial reward amounted to a little less than £200, and the committee felt that they should ask for the assistance of the Government. Their letter to the Secretary of State for the Home Office read:

> At a meeting of the gentlemen of Whitechapel, at 74 Mile End road E. It was resolved to approach you upon the subject of the reward we are about to offer you, for the discovery of the author or authors of the latest attrocities in the East End of London, and to ask you sir, to augment our fund for the said purpose, or kindly relate your reasons for refusal.

A reply to this letter was immediate and emphatic, dated 17 September 1888, it read:

> Sir, I am directed by the Secretary of State to acknowledge receipt of your letter of the 10th inst., with reference to the question of the offer of a reward for the discovery of the perpetrator of the recent murders in Whitechapel, and I am to inform you that, had the Secretary of State considered the case a proper one for the offer of a reward, he would at once have offered one on behalf of the Government, but, that the practice of offering rewards for the discovery of criminals was discontinued some years ago because experience showed that such offers of rewards tended to produce more harm than good, and the Secretary of State is satisfied that there is nothing in the circumstances of the present case to justify a departure from this rule.
>
> Signed
> G.Leigh Pemberton.

Officially this was the correct and only course of action available to the Government. An offer of reward money would mean that the police would be inundated with false leads and suspects from all over the world, thus delaying the investigation further. Since the whole area of Whitechapel/Spitalfields was a known ghetto for the criminal community, it was extremely unlikely that anything but fabricated evidence and untruths would be forthcoming.

The press had a field day with the Government's response to the Vigilance Committee's letter, and attempted to portray it as a direct lack of interest. Matters were made worse when the Lord Mayor of London offered a reward of £500, and a Member of

Parliament offered a further £100. Meanwhile the Vigilance Committee used the £200 they had raised to supplement the cost of hiring two private detectives and to pay for two dozen pairs of galoshes so that the men detailed for patrol duties could do so in silence. A dozen men were paid to patrol designated beats between midnight and 6.00 a.m. Initially, due to a distinct lack of communication, a number of these patrols were arrested by police-officers for acting suspiciously in the streets. Simultaneously, the police had detailed a number of officers to patrol in plain-clothes dressed as a typical East-ender. However, the uniformed patrols were not advised of this fact and numerous embarrassing arrests resulted.

It seemed that almost everyone wanted to become an amateur detective. A large number of independent sleuths took to the streets, talking to the dossers and hawkers in the hope that they would procure vital information. One such individual was Doctor Forbes Winslow, who himself became a latter-day Ripper suspect. Winslow claimed to have spent months on the streets and alleys of the district and often arrived at the scene of the crime before the police. Eventually, Winslow was frightened off by police enquiries into his whereabouts on the nights of some of the murders. Winslow often made dramatic statements to the press. Once he implied he had personal knowledge of the killer's identity, yet when the police questioned him about this he denied ever making such a claim and was never actively involved again. Winslow did much damage to the reputation of the police by his derogatory statements.

With all this hyperactivity, the killer could be forgiven for believing that people had actually forgotten about him. Dramatically he thrust himself into the public eye with the deft movement of a pen which defies all reasoning. On Thursday 27 September 1888 the Central News Agency in London received a letter dated 25 September 1888 and postmarked in the East End of London:

> Dear Boss,
> I keep on hearing the Police have caught me, but they wont fix me just yet. I have laughed when they look so clever and talk about being on the *right* track. That joke about Leather Apron gave me real fits. I am down on whores and shant quit ripping them till I do get buckled. Grand work the last job was, i gave the lady no time to squeal. How can they catch me now, I love my

> work and want to start again, you will soon hear of me with my funny little games, I saved some of the proper red stuff in a ginger beer bottle over the last job to write with but it went thick like glue and I cant use it. Red ink is fit enough I hope *ha ha*. The next job I do I shall clip the ladys ear off and send it to the police officers just for a jolly wouldnt you. Keep this letter back till I do a bit more work then give it out straight. My knifes so nice and sharp I want to get to work right away if I get a chance good luck.
>
> yours truly
> Jack the Ripper

As if that wasn't enough, written across the bottom of the letter at a right angle was, 'Dont mind me giving the trade name. Wasnt good enough to post this before I got all the red ink off my hands, curse it. No luck yet. They say I am a doctor now *ha ha*'.

As one would have expected the letter is in red ink in order to resemble blood and to titillate the sanguinary delights of the public. However, the most striking part of the letter has to be the macabre pseudonym the killer gives himself. Closer inspection of the letter and its wording reveals its author's frame of mind. By his mocking locution he intends to instil fear into prostitutes. There are many grammatical errors and it has been claimed that it has been penned by an educated hand, yet closer inspection reveals that it has been written down as one would speak.

There are certain American colloquialisms contained within the text, such as 'Dear Boss' or 'fix me'. Despite various attempts by authors to link this terminology with America, I categorically state that such language was common enough in England for it to be used by the Ripper. It is a common belief that the author of this letter was in fact a journalist who was known to the police. I fail to agree with this. Numerous persons were arrested and prosecuted for wasting police time during the Ripper investigation and a journalist would have not escaped, especially if the authorities believed he had carried out the biggest hoax ever known to mankind at that time. Furthermore, why did the authorities arrange for thousands of facsimile copies of the letter to be made and distributed throughout London? The authenticity of the letter will always be questioned, yet for a number of reasons I believe it to be authentic. Primarily, because the police of the time held it was true, and secondly, because psychopathic killers often feel the need to publicize their crimes. Jack the Ripper was no different.

The Central News Agency did as the letter requested and refrained from publishing the letter. Soon a second letter was received, this time by the police. Postmarked 'Liverpool, 29 September 1888', the letter read:

> Beware I shall be at work on the first and second in the Minories at twelve midnight, and I give the authorities a good chance, but there is never a policeman near when I am at work.

Quite naturally the authorities were dubious about this second letter and dismissed it as a hoax. In doing so they made a terrible mistake. In the early hours of Sunday 30 September 1888, two more women were found cruelly butchered in Whitechapel. One of the women was found close to the Minories. This has to be pure coincidence for the second letter is a hoax and I believe the police made the right decision in ignoring it. Similarities between the two letters are minimal.

A third letter quickly followed, this time received by the Central News Agency. In this letter, dated 30 September 1888, the author made various claims about his previous night's work:

> I was not codding, dear old boss, when I gave you the tip. You'll hear about saucy Jacks work tomorrow. Double event this time. Number one squealed a bit, couldnt finish straight off. Had no time to get ears for Police. Thanks for keeping last letter back till i got to work again
>
> Signed
> Jack the Ripper

The letter, although dated 30 September, was actually postmarked 1 October 1888. Therefore, it has to be possible that someone was aware of the previous night's activities and the 'Dear Boss' letter which was circulated the same day and could write the third letter. Similarly, it has to be said that the Ripper could have posted it after committing the crimes. Once released by the press, the letters were copied by thousands of people, many of whom wrote to Scotland Yard with wild claims – over a thousand per week were received at one stage. Individual police-officers were tasked with scrutinzing each one, it is from such data that one can establish just how difficult a task the police had.

The handwriting in all three letters is different. The first 'Dear Boss' letter reported information and evidence which were otherwise unknown, only police-officers and doctors being aware of some of the details identified by the author. The second letter is obviously the work of a different party, by this time the press were aware of the name 'Jack the Ripper', as they received the initial letter they would be able to promote further fear and scandal by submitting the second letter. The fact that this mentions the Minories is nothing more than a coincidence. In fact Mitre Square lies in the Aldgate (St James) Ward so the location given is incorrect. The police realized that it was the work of an enterprising journalist, and that they could dismiss it as a hoax. The third letter is in yet another hand. By now many journalists knew of the previous letters and the 'Double Event' was common knowledge among the gentlemen of the press. Even though the letter is dated 30 September 1888 (with the obvious intent that the reader would infer that it was completed immediately after the Mitre Square crime) the actual postmark declares that it was posted on 1 October 1888. Anyone who knew of the 'Double Event' (such as a journalist) could have fabricated the letter in order to cause further panic and sell more papers. These certainly were the official police conclusions since only the 'Dear Boss' letter was taken seriously and investigated further.

The letters' authenticity is one of the main points of conjecture among all Ripperologists. Drawing upon my own experience of such work, I cannot get away from the fact that the initial 'Dear Boss' letter has to be authentic, while the follow-ups are hoaxes. The letters proved that Jack the Ripper was alive and well, and awaiting his next opportunity to prove himself.

Meanwhile, the press resumed their attack on the police. One crazed journalist had the audacity to claim that the Ripper might be from the police ranks. The only occupation not singled out as suspect was that of the journalist! Even today, I feel that journalists are given too much freedom to express their personal opinions and thus influence readers, yet in 1888 such matters were not important. All the public were interested in were the crimes of Jack the Ripper and the ineptitude of the Metropolitan Police.

Elizabeth Stride

The first of the two victims killed by the Ripper on the night of 30 September 1888 was found in Berner Street, which ran north to south off the Commercial Road. It is situated on the fringes of the supposed Ripper area. Berner Street is not a long road, but it has altered drastically since 1888 when it led down to the London, Tilbury and Southend Railway, and is now known as Henriques Street. Like many other roads in 1888, it was lined by tiny two-storey jerry-built houses which were depressing to look at, never mind live in. In 1888, a large school stood on its eastern side which took up most of the street, on the western side of the street stood a few small shops and the International Working Mens Educational Club clubhouse was at No. 40. Running down the south side of the club premises and leading off Berner Street was a small passageway, this led into a tiny yard which was locally known as Dutfields Yard. Two large wooden gates stood at the entrance to the passageway in Berner Street. As a general rule these usually stood open since there were a few small dwelling cottages within the yard and this was the only real point of access for the occupants.

At around 1.00 a.m., Louis Diemschutz turned his pony and trap into Dutfields Yard. Diemschutz was returning from Westow Hill market, Crystal Palace where he had been selling the cheap jewellery which he made. His wife normally remained at the Educational Club to care for the running of the premises as the couple had been official club stewards for about seventeen months. The main patrons of the club were Russian Poles, Jews and those with an interest in socialism. On entering the yard Diemschutz found that his pony appeared to shy away from something and pulled to the left, refusing to proceed any further. Diemschutz looked at the cobbled stones to see what had startled his pony. To his right he could just make out a shape lying upon the damp cobblestones. Tentatively he prodded at the object with his whip, then, remaining uncertain as to its identity, he alighted from the cart and struck a match. In the few seconds that the flame illuminated the dark corners of the tiny area, Diemschutz saw that the form which lay at his feet was that of a woman who was either drunk or dead. At once he rushed into the club in order to confirm his wife's safety. On ascertaining this, he told the club patrons of his find. The intrigued members rushed into the yard. From the light of a candle they saw that the woman was dead, her throat had been cut and blood ran down from the gash in her neck into the gutters towards the back door of the club premises. Diemschutz and another man called Kozobrodski immediately went in search of a police-officer, others ran in the opposite direction with the same intention.

Constable 252H Henry Lamb was walking between Christian Street and Batty Street when he was approached by two extremely agitated men who were screaming and shouting in panic. The bemused constable asked the men what the problem was to which the men blurted out, 'Come on, there has been another murder.'

Lamb hurried back to Berner Street with the two men and on entering Dutfields Yard he saw that a crowd of people had gathered, some of whom were shouting, 'Murder Murder!' The constable calmly switched on his bull's-eye lantern and shone it at the body which lay on the cobbles, the woman lay on her left side with an obvious gash in her throat. Making use of the sightseers, Lamb asked people to go and find doctors and more police-officers. As Lamb stood over the body, trying to assess the incident, he instinctively bent down and felt the woman's face. It was still warm and that meant that the killer could not be far away.

At 1.16 a.m. Doctor Frederick William Blackwell of 100 Commercial Road arrived at the scene. He advised Lamb to close the entrance gates to the yard and to retain all witnesses inside the clubhouse. Meanwhile, Blackwell began his examination of the body noting:

> Body lay on its left side, obliquely across the passage, face looking towards the right wall of passage. Her head was resting on paving slab, beyond carriage wheel rut with her neck lying on the rut. Feet were approximately three feet from gateway. The neck and chest were warm as too the legs and face. The hands were cold, right hand open on chest and smeared in blood, left hand on ground partially open and contained a small packet of cachous, the left arm was extended from the elbow. No rings on fingers, mouth slightly open, deceased had a check silk scarf on, the bow of which had been moved round to the left. A long incision in the neck corresponded with the lower border of the scarf. The border was slightly frayed, as if by a sharp knife.

Bonnet laying by head on left side of body. Estimated that body had been dead for twenty minutes to half an hour.

While this examination was being carried out, Doctor Phillips arrived and assisted in any way he could.

Eventually Inspector Pinhorn arrived and the police enquiries commenced. All patrons of the club were interviewed and a full search of the yard and surrounding premises was carried out. The police found nothing which could remotely be construed as evidence. The body of the mystery victim was removed to St George's-in-the-East mortuary at around 4.30 a.m. Officially, the police had not yet linked this crime with Jack the Ripper, but all that was to change.

A full description of the woman was circulated to all local police stations:

Female, age around 42-45 years, length, five foot two inches. Complexion, pale, dark brown hair (Curly), light grey eyes, upper teeth lost. Wearing old black jacket and skirt, jacket trimmed with black fur. Small bunch of flowers pinned to right side of jacket (Maidenhair fern and red rose), two light serge petticoats, white stockings, white chemise, black side spring boots and black crepe bonnet.

Monday 1 October saw the inquest into the Berner Street victim commence. Coroner Wynne Baxter was once again called to preside over the affair. The same day saw the return to Scotland Yard of Sir Robert Anderson who, on the advice of his doctor, had been away on holiday in Switzerland. Unfortunately for Anderson, his holidays had coincided with the first Whitechapel murder and he had missed the subsequent events. Many newspapers claimed that Anderson had run away in order to escape his responsibilities. On his return he was at once called to attend various high-powered meetings between the Home Office and the police commissioner.

The inquest had in the meantime commenced with incredible ineptitude. Mrs Mary Malcolm, the wife of a Red Lion Square tailor, was called to give evidence. Mrs Malcolm declared that the body she had viewed at the mortuary was that of her sister, Elizabeth Watts. She had recognized the body because of a bite mark which had been received from an adder many years previously. Following this revelation, Malcolm performed a character assassination on the unfortunate woman, informing the inquest of her sister's wild affairs and many illegitimate children. However, other witnesses were called and claimed the body was that of local prostitute Elizabeth Stride. Coroner Baxter adjourned matters until verification of identity could be ascertained. This was confirmed when Constable Walter Frederick Stride of Clapham division identified the body as that of Elizabeth Stride who had been married to his uncle.

Elizabeth Stride was born in Torslanda, Sweden on 27 November 1843. Her maiden name was Gustaafsdotter and her parents were farmers. In 1860 Elizabeth gained employment as a maid in Gothenburg. By 1865 she had been registered by the Swedish authorities as a prostitute. In April of the same year she gave birth to a still-born child and after a brief period of recuperation she returned to the streets. In February 1866 she arrived in London and gained employment as a servant maid near Hyde Park. By now both her parents had died and this may be why she came to London in search of a new life. After a brief courtship with a police-officer, followed by release from her permanent employment, she soon floundered again into a life of prostitution.

In March 1869 she met John Thomas Stride whom she married. Stride was a carpenter by trade, and it is believed that the couple had nine children! As with many of her class, Elizabeth Stride found married life difficult and she could not cope with the stability required. Arguments were constant and Elizabeth attempted to console herself with alcohol. Eventually the couple split up. In March 1877 Elizabeth was in Poplar workhouse, from there she disappears until 28 December 1881 when she was admitted to Whitechapel Infirmary suffering from bronchitis. In January 1882, she was released from the infirmary and returned to life in the workhouse. John Stride passed away in 1884, by which time Elizabeth had become an established prostitute in Whitechapel. She often returned to 32 Flower and Dean Street where she had met her husband. Elizabeth struck up another relationship, this time with a waterside labourer known as Michael Kidney. The couple resided at 35 Dorset Street, where Annie Chapman had lived prior to her death. Together the couple lived quite happily at this address, although occasionally Elizabeth would disappear for a few days

Death of Nicholls

Essex Wharf, Bucks Row (now renamed Durward Street), where Polly Nicholls fell victim

he Nicholls murder site lies pposite the iron railing gates Essex Wharf

Looking along Bucks Wharf. The entrance to the murder site is on the left

Bucks Row. Corrugated iron conceals the only Ripper murder site still in existence

It was behind this bedroom window, view from the murder site in Bucks Row, that Mrs Walter Purkess spent a sleepless night, her husband was also awak tending to her. The pres of the day made a great deal out of the fact that Mrs Purkess lay awake

A copycat attack

Until now it was believed that George Yard Buildings, where Martha Turner/ Tabram was murdered, had been destroyed. Here is a unique photograph of the scene of that first attack which inspired the Ripper to kill

Another previously unpublished photograph. Gunthorpe Street, site of George Yard Buildings and better known then as the appositely named Shit Alley

29 Hanbury Street. The Ripper led Annie Chapman through the door on the left

The rear yard of 29 Hanbury Street where Eliza Ann Chapman was found dead, with her head lying by the wall between the stone steps and the fence at a time, this was either in a bout of drunkenness or in the course of prostitution.

Michael Kidney gave evidence at the inquest informing the authorities that between 9 or 10 p.m. on the night of 27 September 1888 he had been on his way home from work when he met 'Liz' in Commercial Street. He claimed this was the last time he had seen her alive.

Another witness, Elizabeth Tanner, the deputy of 32 Flower and Dean Street lodgings told how she had attended the mortuary and recognized the body as that of 'Long Liz' whom she had known personally for six years. During that time Liz had often claimed that her husband and two young children had perished in the *Princess Alice* pleasure-steamer disaster of 1878. (Despite thorough research, I cannot find any reference to the name of Stride in the list of dead passengers who perished in the disaster. Elizabeth Stride was a fantasist who could not contain herself to the truth. Her ordinary background was not to her liking and she told many stories which have no factual evidence to support them.) Liz had returned to 32 Flower and Dean Street on the night of 27 September and requested two nights accommodation since she had fallen out with her man.

The police pieced together all the snippets of information they had received through their enquiries and drew up an account of Liz Stride's last twenty-four hours. On Saturday 29 September 1888 she had been drinking in the Queen's Head public house, Commercial Street with Elizabeth Tanner. Later they returned to 32 Flower and Dean Street where Liz cleaned Tanner's room for sixpence. Catherine Lane, a fellow lodger, saw her in the kitchen of the same lodgings at around 7 p.m. that day. At 11 p.m. she was sighted in the company of a man with a dark moustache and billycock hat, the couple had just left the Bricklayers public house in North Commercial Street and walked to a darkened doorway where they entwined in a passionate embrace. Two labourers saw the courting couple and made fun of them, cursing them, Liz Stride and her partner departed in the general direction of Berner Street. At 11.45 p.m. William Marshall of 64 Berner Street saw Liz Stride on the pavement opposite 58 Berner Street. Marshall could not provide a full description of her companion, but believed that he was wearing a black cutaway coat, dark trousers and a round cap with a peak. He looked somewhat like an office clerk. The couple remained there for some time, talking and kissing. The companion was overheard to say, 'You would say anything but your prayers' and at this comment the couple had burst out laughing.

Local greengrocer Matthew Packer also alleged he had seen the couple, claiming that they had entered his Berner Street shop around midnight. The man bought half a pound of black grapes and then left the shop.

A similar sighting of an identical couple was made by Israel Schwartz of 22 Helen Street. Schwartz had been passing through Berner Street at around 12.45 a.m. Outside Dutfields Yard he saw a man stop a woman and speak to her, the man treated the woman very roughly and swung her round and on to the ground and the woman had screamed out. Not wishing to become involved, Schwartz crossed the street and saw that he was being watched by a second man. The woman's attacker shouted to Schwartz, 'Lipski, Lipski', but he fled from the scene in fear of being mugged by the assailants of the unfortunate woman. The word 'Lipski' was an insult to all Jews since a Jew named Lipski had poisoned a woman. It was a cowardly murder and the local Jewish community disowned him and refused to support him in his hour of need.

Police Constable 452H William Smith saw a couple in Berner Street just before 12.45 a.m. The woman was leaning against a wall and her companion was facing her with his left arm leaning against the same wall.

The descriptions were similar, it appeared that the police had substantial information at last. The following description was inserted in the *Police Gazette*:

> At 12.35 a.m., 30 September 1888 with Elizabeth Stride found murdered on the same date in Berner street at 0100 a.m. a man age [*sic*] twenty eight, height 5ft 8ins, complexion dark, small dark moustache, dress – black diagonal coat, hard felt hat, collar and tie, respectable appearance, carried a parcel wrapped in newspaper.

The inquest heard all the available evidence from witnesses and police-officers alike, and Coroner Wynne Baxter commenced his summing-up of the death of Elizabeth Stride on 24 October 1888. He reminded the jury of the injuries to Stride's neck and how the windpipe had been severed causing the mass effusion of blood. Baxter referred to another crime which had been committed within an hour of the Stride murder and had taken place in Mitre Square. The jury returned a typical verdict of murder by some person or persons unknown.

Elizabeth Stride was buried at the East London cemetery in grave No. 15509.

The second death which is reputed to have been caused by the same killer of Elizabeth Stride had occurred on the City of London Police Force's patch. The City boys now had the opportunity they had eagerly awaited for some time. All too often they had slated the Metropolitan's handling of the case, inferring that they were better equipped to handle matters. It was now up to them to prove the point, but it might not be easy.

Catharine Eddowes

The second murder committed on the night of 30 September 1888 was more familiar than that in Berner Street which lacked any kind of mutilation. The crime was committed in Mitre Square which lay just behind St Katherine Cree Church in Leadenhall Street, Aldgate. The square had three points of access. Two sides of the cobbled area were surrounded by the warehouses of Kearley and Tonge teamakers, during the hours of darkness these premises were protected by George James Morris who acted as night-watchman. The other sides of the square were taken up by various dwelling-houses, the majority of which were empty. One of the few families who resided within the square were the Pearses, Richard Pearse being employed as a Metropolitan police constable. The patrolling police-officer entered Mitre Square every fifteen minutes or so whilst on his beat, and another constable regularly patrolled the Duke Street entrance. It was what could be classed as a secure area.

Police Constable 881 Edward Watkins was detailed the Mitre Square patrol by his duty sergeant on the commencement of his night-shift on 29 September 1888. The adjoining beat was detailed to Constable James Harvey. Edward Watkins passed through Mitre Square at around 1.30 a.m. on the morning of Sunday 30 September 1888 and, finding nothing unusual or of any interest, continued along his beat. The constable must have been aware of the commotion which had occurred somewhere along the Commercial Road, the Metropolitan boys were having it rough, and Watkins knew that he was lucky not to have joined the City's other force. Through his friendship with some of the Metropolitan lads, he knew of their anger over the apparent mismanagement of the force. Some five minutes after Watkins left the square, James Harvey walked along Church Passage and into the south-west corner of the square. Scouring the confines of the square, Harvey was unable to locate Watkins, so he resumed his normal beat patrol along Duke Street. The City Police had been told that they should stop any woman whom they met walking alone after midnight and advise her to go home. This instruction was ignored by the majority of officers who felt it an almost impossible task to discuss such procedures with the type of women they came across during their patrols.

At 1.44 a.m., for the fifteenth time that particular shift, Edward Watkins entered Mitre Square. Somewhat complacently, Watkins raised his bull's-eye lantern and shone it into the corners of the square and as he walked, via the south-west entrance he received the shock of his life, for there on the pavement was the horribly disfigured form of a woman who had been butchered. Watkins later described the woman as 'being ripped up like a pig'.

In a state of massive confusion, Watkins ran for the assistance of George Morris the local night-watchman, who coincidentally had been a police-officer. 'For God's sake, man, come to my assistance,' cried Watkins. Morris walked over to the body and at once blew on a whistle to summon assistance, he found the injuries too much to comprehend in one go and walked into Mitre Street. Constable James Harvey heard the commotion and ran to the scene where Watkins told him to go to Bishopsgate police station and request help. This message was received by the duty inspector Edward Collard who sent two constables to inform Doctor Sequira of Jewry Street and Gordon Brown of Finsbury Circus, the official divisional surgeon, of the murder. Major Henry Smith was informed of the incident at Cloak Lane police station, Southwark, and hurried to the scene using a hansom cab. Major Smith was the acting commissioner of the City of London Force. He took an active interest in the Ripper crimes and deemed it a contest between the Metropolitan Force and his own to catch the perpetrator. He often slept overnight at City police stations in the locality in case a crime occurred in their district. Police-officers had orders that on such occasions he was to be called to the scene without delay, hence his appearance in Goulston Street, he had in fact been sleeping at Cloak Lane police station that very evening. His enthusiasm to locate the Ripper was by far the greatest of any senior police official of that time.

Doctor Sequira was the first official to arrive shortly before two o'clock, he declined to touch the body until the arrival of the divisional surgeon which delayed matters by some twenty-five minutes. Inspector Collard instructed numerous constables to carry out thorough searches of all lodging-houses etc.

Sergeant Jones carried out a search of the square and found three small black buttons of the kind usually found on boots, one small metal button, a common metal thimble and a small metal mustard tin which contained two pawn tickets, these were handed to Inspector Collard.

After pronouncing life extinct, the doctors instructed that the body be removed to Golden Lane mortuary where they would carry out a more detailed examination. The officials declared that the murder had been committed within the hour, as blood had dripped from the wounds inflicted on to the pavement, that the blood had not yet congealed implied that the crime was recent. Typically, Doctor Sequira claimed that the murderer would have had insufficient light to commit the crime within Mitre Square. Doctor Brown noted in his official report:

> The body was on its back, the head turned to the left shoulder, the arms by the side of the body as if they had fallen there, both palm upwards, the fingers slightly bent. A thimble was lying off the finger on the right side.

The woman had been the victim of the most horrific attack most of the police-officers present had ever seen. Her clothes had been drawn up above the abdomen and both thighs were naked. The left leg was extended in a line with the body, the right leg was bent at the thigh and the knee. The abdomen was exposed and there was terrible disfigurement to the facial area, with Vs cut into each cheek, a slice removed from her nose and cuts across the eyelids. The throat had been cut straight across severing most of the main arteries. The intestines were drawn out to a large extent, with some being strewn over the woman's right shoulder, they were smeared with some feculent matter. A piece of intestine had become detached from the body and had been dropped between the body and the left arm. The lobe and auricle of the left ear were cut obliquely through. The ears were not, despite various claims, missing, they had been quite cleanly cut. A quantity of blood was evident around the neck and body areas, blood had also been smeared on the woman's arms and thighs. There was no evidence of any sexual interference.

The body was removed to the Golden Lane mortuary and the two doctors and Inspector Collard followed. All officers concerned immediately realized that they were dealing with another victim of the Whitechapel murderer.

Dozens of different police-officers searched the local lodging-houses, but no clues were evident, once again no one gave any cause for suspicion. Detective Halse of the City CID commenced his search of the adjoining streets, gradually he worked his way eastwards, across Houndsditch and Middlesex Street and into Goulston Street from its southernmost end. By this point, Halse had crossed the boundaries of his jurisdiction and saw that the uniform branch of the Metropolitan Force was carrying out a similar task to that of his own force. Halse returned to Mitre Square where he was advised that a piece of the dead woman's apron was missing having been cut with a sharp-bladed implement. The missing piece was found in a doorway in Goulston Street. Detective Halse rushed to the scene, his enthusiasm flowing and adrenalin pumping around his body at an alarming rate. On his arrival at the scene he saw a number of uniformed Metropolitan boys standing in doorway 108–119 of Wentworth Dwellings. The detective constable was convinced that he had earlier witnessed these doorways being checked by the Metropolitan Force and he could not understand why the piece of apron had not been found earlier that morning. For the time being Halse chose to remain silent and assess the situation.

The apron had been found by Constable Alfred Long of A division, Metropolitan Force, who had recently been seconded to the district to assist with patrols. Long informed his seniors that he had checked the area at 2.20 a.m. but had found nothing untoward present, however, on his return at 2.55 a.m. he found the piece of apron on the floor of the doorway to Wentworth

Dwellings. Above the apron someone had chalked upon a wall in red chalk, 'The Juwes are the men that will not be blamed for nothing'. The writing was in a typical schoolboy hand and individual letters were approximately one inch high. The commissioners of both forces were called to attend. Meanwhile, Halse did his best to protect what he believed to be vital evidence.

Superintendent Arnold of the Metropolitan Force arrived and read the writing. Having done so, he immediately instructed that it be erased in its entirety. It is believed he decided on this course of action because of the number of Jews who lived in the area and the fear of an uprising. Before any further action could be taken, acting superintendent McWilliam of the City Force arrived and requested that the message be covered over until it was light enough for it to be photographed. Arnold refused and demanded the message be erased. He then sent word to Sir Charles Warren informing him of the situation. After a farcical two hours, during which all kinds of ridiculous arguments took place, Sir Charles arrived and at 5.00 a.m. he personally erased the message in order to confirm his loyalty to his subordinate officer. The City Force were furious and demanded an explanation. Warren refused to broach the subject, knowing full well that his actions would be condemned, but confident that he was correct.

By now the whole area of Whitechapel and Spitalfields was swarming with police-officers. Two officers found a sink off Dorset Street down which bloody water had run. It was a strange find and one which clearly gives some indication as to the direction the killer took during his escape from the scene. The blood was fresh and police believed it to be one of the locations where the killer had stopped to rinse his hands. This fact becomes more certain when one realizes just how few people would walk into one of London's most roughest streets, covered in blood, and wash their hands in a public sink. There were no slaughterhouses in the immediate area so who would be likely to wash their bloody hands in the sink? Only a local man would dare to head directly for Dorset Street as no stranger would dare enter within its confines. A local would realize that Dorset Street would provide excellent sanctuary since it was too obvious a place to hide.

Many people have made a great deal of the writing on the wall in Goulston Street. The majority believe Sir Charles Warren made a great error in erasing it. Yet, could the message have been written by Jack the Ripper? According to police patrol times, the Mitre Square murder took place between 1.35 and 1.44 a.m. This allows the killer just nine minutes to commit his crime. Having just completed his most horrendous crime to date, he crossed Houndsditch and Middlesex Street before arriving in Goulston Street. Dozens of police-officers must have been converging on the tiny district at that particular time. The time it took to walk from Mitre Square to Goulston Street was officially recorded by the police as eight minutes. The killer, fleeing from the scene of his crime, would walk rather quickly to avoid being caught, so at 1.45 a.m. Jack the Ripper would have left Mitre Square arriving in Goulston Street at 1.55 a.m. at the latest. Are we then to believe that he hung around Goulston Street for a further one hour and ten minutes before depositing the bloody piece of apron in the doorway and calmly taking the time to scrawl a message which mocked the authorities – all this while the streets and alleys were crawling with searching police-officers? Jack the Ripper was no fool, he would not take unnecessary risks by loitering in the very vicinity where he had just committed one of his most dastardly crimes.

Somewhere the timing of these events has to be incorrect. It may well be that Constable Long missed the piece of apron on his earlier search. This can be put down to human error, none of us are perfect and Alfred Long most certainly was not. Some nine months after the affair, he was found to be drunk on duty and dismissed from the force. It is not for me to speculate upon Constable Long's condition that particular September morning, but it is recorded that he was not fully conversant with all that he found then and the coroner was later to complain of Long's sincerity in giving evidence.

Much has been made of the writing on the wall in the Wentworth Dwellings in Goulston Street. The favourite theory regularly expounded refers to the writing being of 'masonic' influence. The word 'Juwes' is interpreted as connected with the mythical tale of Jubela, Jebelum and Jubelo, the three traitors who murdered Hiram Abiff near the Temple of Solomon. Sir Charles Warren was a Royal Arch Mason, one of the highest ranking masons in the land, and some would have us believe that this meant he was untouchable in the eyes of the law. This is pure conjecture. If the Ripper murders did have any connection with freemasonry, then why did Sir Charles's brothers in the force fail to inform him of the fact and cause him severe embarrassment? Loyalty to a fellow mason is one of the most important principles of the organization so a number of rules must have been broken, but for what reason?

Sir Charles Warren has been castigated by many for his actions in Goulston Street that fateful morning, yet few are qualified to comment on the matter. Initially it appears that the writing was anti-Semitic propaganda, perhaps chalked by someone with a grievance towards the Jewish community. It cannot be construed as a statement from a killer, nor as a red herring scrawled in an attempt to mislead the authorities. Having many personal friends among the various ranks of the Metropolitan Police, I was able to speak at length with various officers regarding the mystery of the writing found in Goulston Street. Although the views raised during such discussions are the personal opinions of latter-day policemen, they do give a slightly different interpretation of the proceedings of that September morning in 1888. Indeed I have heard the story so many times that I am now inclined to believe it rather than the weak solutions previously given.

With much ill feeling between the respective forces apparent throughout all ranks, many cutting or sarcastic comments were flying around. Matters had not been helped by the media's insistence that the Metropolitan Police alone were to blame for everything that was wrong in the East End. The news of Jack the Ripper's fourth murder spread around the area quickly on that September morning. It was also common knowledge that the victim had been allowed to wander from the sanctuary of a City Police station and to her death in Mitre Square. She was still drunk when released and should never have been released from the cells, but this irregularity was never pressed and the City Police escaped the criticism they deserved. However, the officers on the ground made a great deal of the saga and it seems probable that one officer left his beat in Whitechapel and went to Wentworth Street where he wrote the message which was to become legendary. The message was nothing more than a jibe at the City Police. The word 'Juwes' should have been spelt 'Jewes' and was meant to refer to the nickname used by the majority of the Metropolitan Officers when referring to their City opponents. The nickname derives from the Old Jewry police headquarters of the City Police.

If the story is correct, a fact in which I have no reason to doubt, then it explains Superintendent Arnold and Sir Charles Warren's rival actions in removing the message.

The writing on the wall in Goulston Street cannot be conclusively linked with the murders. This is the first of the so-called mysteries to which I found a simple and effective solution. Detective work is often straightforward and if one looks too deeply then the matter becomes clouded by data of no relevance, sadly it seems that the mystery surrounding Jack the Ripper has been self-induced.

There were no official photographs taken of the writing. However, Doctor Thomas Dutton, an expert in micro-photography claims to have owned a selection of prints which he took at the time at the request of the police. He further claimed that the negatives were destroyed by Scotland Yard, but he retained several copies for himself. Dutton expressed an opinion that there was a direct similarity between the writing in Goulston Street and that of the 'Dear Boss' letter. A direct copy of the Goulston Street writing can be found in the Home Office files on the case which are held at the Public Records Office (private letters file), in the form of a memorandum from Sir Charles Warren to the Secretary of State. Personal and expert opinions allow me to state that no such similarity is evident, there is no professional graphologist in the world who would make such a claim. The question is whether the writing would have been linked with the murders if the piece of apron had not been found beneath it? The answer to this has to be no. The walls and doorways of such buildings were just as likely to be covered with vast quantities of graffiti covering a wide variety of topics as the slums of today. The message on the wall then was of no real relevance to the Ripper enquiry.

The body of the Mitre Square victim arrived at the Golden Lane mortuary and Inspector Collard busily scribbled down an inventory of the woman's personal possessions and clothing: black straw bonnet, trimmed with green and black velvet and black beads with black strings. Black cloth jacket, imitation fur edging around the collar, fur round sleeves. Chintz skirt, three flounces brown button on waistband. Brown linsey dress bodice, black velvet collar, brown metal buttons down front.

Grey stuff petticoat, white waistband. Very old green Alpaca skirt. Very old ragged blue skirt, red flounces, light twill lining. White calico chemise, man's white vest button to match down front, two outside pockets. Pair of men's lace-up boots, mohair laces, right boot repaired with red thread. One piece of red gauze silk. One large white handkerchief. Two unbleached calico pockets, tape string and top left corner cut off one. One blue strip bed-ticking pocket, all strings cut through (all three pockets). One white cotton pocket handkerchief with red-and-white bird's-eye border. One pair of brown ribbed stockings, feet mended in white. Twelve pieces of white rag. One piece of white coarse linen. One piece of blue-and-white shirting, two small bed-ticking bags. One tin box containing tea. One tin box containing sugar. One piece of flannel and six pieces of soap. One small toothcomb. One white-handled table-knife and one metal teaspoon. One red leather cigarette-case, white metal fittings. One tin matchbox, empty. One mustard tin containing two pawntickets. One piece of red flannel containing pins and needles. One ball of hemp and one piece of old white apron. This was all that remained of the dead woman's possessions, all that remained of her life, contained within her torn and filthy clothing. Doubtless she wore three tattered skirts and a petticoat in a hopeless attempt to keep warm. It seemed an impossible task to identify anyone from such belongings, but such clues can often be helpful if read correctly.

The pawntickets which had been found in the mustard tin were traced to a Mr Jones of Church Street, Spitalfields, the recipient was Emily Birrel/Anne Kelly and had been issued against one man's shirt and a pair of boots. The police soon established the victim's identity, the address listed on the rear of the pawntickets was 6 Dorset Street, and it was from such data that the police were able to build a picture of the dead woman's past.

She had been arrested at around 8.00 p.m. on Saturday 29 September 1888, standing in the middle of Bishopsgate doing an impression of a fire-engine. She was taken to Bishopsgate police station where she gave her name as Mary Ann Kelly of 6 Fashion Street, and Agnes Smith of 35 Dorset Street. Catharine Eddowes was not unique in attempting to cover up her real identity from the police. It was common practice for prostitutes to give false names and addresses as it made life difficult for the prosecution, especially when it came to locating the women who flitted from address to address with alarming frequency. To give a false name ensured that the authorities would eventually search for the wrong culprit. The police officially believed Eddowes was called Mary Ann Kelly. In this case it would seem that Eddowes may have forgotten which alias she had previously used. Some forty-five minutes later she was locked in her cell. She was released at around 1.00 a.m. still drunk, but having created so much noise that it was decided to let her out to gain some peace! Forty-five minutes after her release she was dead, the City Police more or less delivered her into the hands of the Ripper. The post-mortem on 30 September was performed by Doctor Brown, others present included Doctors Sequira, Phillips and Sedgwick Saunders who was the City analyst. The body was washed down by the mortuary attendant and the post-mortem commenced. Bruising was noted on the shins and rear of the left hand, the hands and the arms were tanned from exposure to the sun. The doctors all concluded that she had been murdered on the spot with no signs of a struggle. A six-to-seven-inch gash ran from one side of the throat to the other, with the blade of the knife passing so deeply that it actually scratched invertebrae. The jugular vein had been opened an inch-and-a-half and the left carotid artery had been severed. The front walls of the abdomen had been opened from the pubis up to the breastbone. The incision ran upwards and had failed to penetrate the skin over the sternum. Various cuts were made to the liver and surrounding tissue. The navel had been cut open leaving a tongue of skin. Another incision had divided the lower abdomen and went half an inch behind the rectum. The left kidney had been removed and the renal artery was cut through by about three quarters of an inch. The womb had been abstracted as had some ligaments. The Ripper had struck with absolute ferocity, yet the injuries sustained were curiously artistic, leaving the victim with the facial appearance of a clown. The Ripper displayed little anatomical knowledge and it transpired that he actually severed the anal artery, covering his knife in faecal matter, and this is possibly why he cut a piece from the woman's apron so that he could wipe his hands and knife.

Amazingly, Doctor Brown claimed that the killer displayed some anatomical knowledge and skill. However Doctor

Saunders believed no skill was required to carry out the said mutilations and Doctor Sequira stated that he did not believe the killer to possess a great degree of medical knowledge and insisted that the injuries could well have been inflicted by a butcher or slaughterman. Eventually, Doctor Brown changed his opinion and agreed with Sequira. None of the doctors were ever unanimous about any one decision made by a colleague, indeed Doctor Brown only agreed with Doctor Phillips' suggestions from etiquette and loyalty since they were both personal friends and professional colleagues.

Monday 1 October 1888 saw the contents of various Ripper letters being released by the press, particular detail was given to the 'Dear Boss' missive. Varied details of Jack's previous night's work were given to an agitated public, and for the people of Whitechapel and Spitalfields the nightmare continued. The publication of the Ripper letters led to a barrage of mail being received by the authorities as well as the press. Police were accused of sleeping on the job and, in particular, Sir Charles Warren was tortured with many scathing remarks. The Metropolitan Force suffered the brunt of the criticism, the press failed to acknowledge the fact that it was the City Force who had bungled the previous night's affairs.

Major Henry Smith and the officers of the City Force were more determined than ever to catch the miscreant who was running amok in the East End and bring him to justice. Systematically, the City Force were forced to draw the same conclusions as the Metropolitan boys in that, with no new evidence being found, the identity of the killer remained a complete mystery. Even though the City Force had less to go on than the Metropolitan Force, each press report released was done so to give the impression that greater knowledge was being retained for security reasons. Major Smith had indeed profited by the Metropolitan Force's earlier mistakes.

The Mitre Square enquiry continued. Various people came forward to identify the dead woman. A group of women viewed the body and believed it to be that of a fellow prostitute, but failed to provide an identity. One woman believed that the deceased was often without financial aid and could regularly be seen sleeping in the toilets to the rear of Dorset Street.

Late in the evening of 2 October, John Kelly, a local labourer, walked into the main foyer of Bishopsgate police station and informed the duty officer that he knew the identity of the Mitre Square victim. Kelly went on to tell the police that whilst reading a newspaper report on the crime, his attention had been drawn to the name of 'Emily Birrell'. Kelly was taken to the mortuary where he viewed the body and positively identified it as being that of Catharine Eddowes/Catharine Conway, he confirmed that one of her boots had been repaired with red cotton, he himself had carried out these repairs. The police interviewed Kelly at great length and recorded as much detail about the dead woman as possible.

John Kelly met Catharine Conway/Eddowes/Kelly seven years before her death in the lodgings at 55 Flower and Dean Street. She was 46 years old having been born in Gaisley Green, Wolverhampton on 14 April 1842. The family had moved to Bermondsey, London, some time later. It was not long before both parents died, leaving twelve children behind. At 19 years of age Kate left home and returned to Birmingham where she lived with her aunt for a short time. Soon she met a soldier by the name of Thomas Conway, his initials were tattooed on her forearm, the couple never married but three children were born of the relationship. In 1880 the couple split up because of Kelly's flirtatious habits. One year later, John Kelly met her in the doss-house.

In early September 1888, Kelly and Eddowes/Conway went hop picking in Kent. News of the Lord Mayor of London's reward travelled to Maidstone and was given immediate attention by Kelly's partner who claimed she had a sneaking suspicion as to the identity of the killer and persuaded Kelly to return with her so that the evidence could be procured and the reward claimed. Whether this was just opportunism or whether she harboured a genuine belief must remain a mystery, but something must have led her to believe that she knew something of importance since everyone knew that the reward money could not be obtained easily.

The couple began the long walk back to London and on their travels met with a woman called 'Emily Birrell' who had given them a pawn ticket for a flannel shirt valued at 9d., the ticket was later identified as one of those contained within the mustard tin found near the body. On Thursday 27 September the couple arrived back in London, penniless and homeless, they somehow managed to scrape together enough money to gain lodgings for one night. The following day the couple found themselves in the same predicament so Kelly gave his partner his boots to pawn which raised half-a-crown. Foolishly, the couple spent most of this money on alcohol, leaving just 6d. to find lodgings for the night. Eddowes gave Kelly the 4d. required for his bed. She spent the evening in the casual ward at Mile End, this was a wise move since females were given better treatment in such places. The couple met again on Saturday 29 September and after a brief search for employment they ate a small meal and parted at 2.00 p.m. Eddowes/Conway intended to go to Bermondsey to see her daughter in order to scrounge money, Kelly was to continue his search for employment. The couple arranged to meet at 4.00 p.m. John Kelly never saw his partner alive again, typically she had failed to keep her final appointment with him. Kelly stayed at 55 Flower and Dean Street that night where he was advised by another resident that he had seen Eddowes being arrested in Bishopsgate earlier. Believing her to be safe in police custody, Kelly felt content that Eddowes would at least have a bed for the night. Later, when the news of the latest Jack the Ripper atrocities became known, he visited the murder sites totally unaware of the fact that his girl was the Mitre Square victim. The six hours between 2.00 p.m. and 8.00 p.m. were missing from Eddowes' life, but little could have occurred during that time since she was later drunk in Bishopsgate.

The City Police made all such evidence available to Coroner Langham on the opening day of the inquest, Thursday 4 October 1888.

The Coroner's court at Golden Lane was filled to capacity. Those present included, Major Smith and Superintendent Foster from the City Force and Mr Crawford the solicitor.

The first witness called was Eliza Gold of Thrawl Street, who informed the Court that after viewing the body at the mortuary she could confirm it as being her sister, who had never been married but was having a relationship with a man named Kelly. John Kelly was the next person to give evidence, amazingly he claimed to have no knowledge of his partner's immoral habits. A commercial traveller, Joseph Lawende who had been with his friends Harry Harris and Joseph Hyam Levy on the night of the murder told how they had left the Imperial Club in Duke Street, and at approximately 1.00 a.m. had seen a man and woman talking in Church Passage, Mitre Square. Lawende was the only one who paid any kind of attention to the courting couple, and said that the female had placed her hand upon the man's chest as they stood facing each other. A full description of the man was furnished, it is almost certainly that of Jack the Ripper. Lawende said the man was aged about thirty, approximately 5 feet 7 inches tall, with a fair complexion, a fair moustache and of medium build. He was dressed in a pepper-and-salt coloured loose jacket, a grey cloth cap with a peak of the same material, a reddish neckerchief tied in knot, and he had the appearance of a sailor.

Coroner Langham made a great deal of the fact that Lawende's two friends had failed to pay any attention to the courting couple; Joseph Levy, in particular, bore the brunt of the criticism. The unfortunate Levy was most apprehensive when spoken to by the coroner in court, which is understandable when one realizes that a courtroom is not the best of places to receive verbal chastisement. Due to Lawende's description of the man as having the appearance of a sailor, all boats and ships entering or exiting the docks area were subjected to a strict search. Further to this, Queen Victoria suggested that all sailors should be questioned including the crews of all cargo ships and cattle boats. No positive results were gleaned from this exercise. Doctor Brown was cross-examined by Mr Crawford as he told of the injuries sustained during and after the attack. Brown told the Court that in his opinion the woman had been murdered while lying down and the mutilations were committed with the killer kneeling at the right side of the woman's body. Such information was not regarded as important, however the press made much of the fact that Brown believed that sufficient light had been available for the killer to see what he was doing and that the mutilations would have taken no more than five minutes to commit.

While the inquest was taking place, Catharine Eddowes was being interred at Ilford cemetery. A strong contingent of City police-officers escorted the cortège to the City boundaries on a cold damp early October morning. On arrival at Old Street, the Metropolitan Police continued the escort under the ever-watchful eye of Inspector Barnham. The cortège passed

Whitechapel church, along Mile End Road and through Bow and Stratford, and eventually arrived at Ilford cemetery. Literally hundreds of people lined the streets in sympathy, women wept and men lowered their heads in respect. The press claimed that over 500 people were present at the funeral. Slowly and deliberately Catharine Eddowes was lowered into the ground, her final public appearance complete.

On Friday 12 October the inquest on her death was completed with a verdict of 'wilful murder by some person or persons unknown' being officially recorded.

The press were working overtime, Jack the Ripper was the biggest event to occur in London for many a day. In total command of a captive audience the press made mass condemnations of the police daily, ridiculous allegations were directed at many senior police officials, particularly Sir Charles Warren. The *Daily Telegraph* of 3 October 1888 reviewed the latest atrocities and commented:

> Although no clue has been secured Mr McWilliam, Chief of the City Police detectives does not despair. He has the reputation of not being easily discouraged, and the City of London detectives have an advantage over the Scotland Yard officers, for they are not tempted to drop one inquiry when a fresh startling event in a measure supersedes the earlier crimes. Mr McWilliam has an able staff at his command and the City uniform Police are an intelligent sort of men, willing and able, if necessary, to render efficient assistance to the Detective department.

This was a typical assessment of the policing as seen by journalists. The police had become political stooges, pawns to the press and public alike. One officer retaliated and made efforts to redeem police confidence by replying to a national newspaper, the *Illustrated Police News* using the pseudonym 'Bloodhound'. For doing this he was sacked. Although 'Bloodhound's' real identity was never released, my own investigations led me to believe he was an officer named Galway. It had now become unbearably agonizing for Metropolitan officers to patrol the East End in the eyes of the public even their own hierarchy had refused to support them.

Sir Charles Warren was well aware of the Force's predicament and to his credit attempted to improve matters. He wrote to various press agencies, and the following account was published in the *Illustrated Police News*:

> Charles Warren points out that the fact that detectives engaged in connection with the Whitechapel murders were following up clues without circumstances coming to the attention of the public, showed that they were doing their work in a proper fashion. Scotland Yard is in fact alert day and night, making as little noise as possible. Everyday the authorities receive 'Information' which is never regarded as too trivial to be passed over without consideration.

Despite such claims by the commissioner, no one took anything he said seriously. The minds of the public had been poisoned by newspaper reports.

In a final attempt to gain some kind of respect, Warren requested that two bloodhounds belonging to Mr Edwin Brough of Scarborough be brought to Scotland Yard for trials. The animals were tested in Regent's Park early one morning and successfully tracked a baiter over a distance of one mile, this was made more difficult by the fact that the ground was covered in a hoar frost. The commissioner was most impressed by the dogs and publicly proclaimed their arrival at the Yard. Negotiations between Mr Brough and Scotland Yard took place for the purchase of the dogs, but no satisfactory agreement could be reached. The dogs' owner found it difficult to insure the dogs when they were being used by Scotland Yard since they were searching in a violent area for the most vicious criminal known to mankind. Finally, late in October, the dogs were tested once again. This time Tooting Common was the chosen venue where for some inexplicable reason the dogs became lost. Warren was again humiliated. Telegrams were sent to all Metropolitan Police stations, and the dogs were eventually recovered.

Back on the streets, the Whitechapel Vigilance Committee was still hard at work. George Lusk was trying to raise public and press interest. Eventually Lusk, like so many others, became a mere pawn of the press who in return gave him a false sense of power and importance. George Lusk became so prominent in newspaper reports that on Tuesday 16 October he personally received correspondence from a person alleging to be the Ripper. It came in the form of a cardboard box which was hand-delivered to his home in Alderney Road. Contained within the box was what appeared to be a human kidney along with another missive:

> From Hell.
>
> Mr Lusk,
>
> Sir, I send you half the kidne I took from one woman, prasarved it for you, tother piece I fried and ate it, was very nice, I may send you the blody knif that took it out if you only wate a whil longer.
>
> Signed,
>
> Catch Me When You Can Mr Lusk.

This particular letter has been analysed and scrutinized by all manner of authorities and it is claimed to be in the hand of somebody with academic qualifications who has made an attempt to disguise the fact. For example, anyone who knows the correct spelling of knife using a 'K' and an 'N' yet misses the 'E' is not as illiterate as he would have us believe. A similar word which is not spelt incorrectly is 'piece'. The writing does not, in any manner or form, resemble the other so-called 'Ripper Letters'.

To his credit, Lusk dismissed the kidney as a hoax and chose to believe that it originated from an animal. Lusk informed the police and the press of the package. Major Smith of the City Police took the kidney to Doctor Openshaw at the London Hospital Museum and requested that he carry out a thorough examination of the piece. Openshaw did as was asked and reported: 'It was a portion of human kidney, and had been placed in spirit within hours of its removal.' The doctor also claimed that it was a 'Ginny Kidney' belonging to a woman of about forty-five years and had been removed from a body within the past three weeks. To this apparently accurate assessment Major Smith added, 'The renal artery is three inches long, two inches of renal artery were found in the body of Eddowes and one inch was attached to the kidney.' The major believed the kidney to be authentic.

Other more qualified authorities were not so keen to accept Doctor Openshaw's conclusions. Doctor Saunders was adamant and correct in stating that there is no difference between a male and a female human kidney. He had been present at the post-mortem of Catharine Eddowes and was aware that the right kidney was in a healthy condition, consequently he questioned whether the left kidney would be infected in the way claimed by Openshaw. Medical officers were in total disagreement with Openshaw's findings and conclusions. When one puts this into perspective, it soon becomes apparent that Openshaw may well have been influenced by press reports and pressures from the hierarchy of the City Police to produce the results which they required. It must be added that at no time were the remains of Catharine Eddowes exhumed which would have conclusively proved whether the amount of renal artery remaining in the body matched that of the mysterious kidney.

On Monday 22 October the City Police received a surprise visitor to their Old Jewry headquarters in the form of Thomas Conway, Catharine Eddowes' first common-law husband. Conway apologised for not reporting sooner, but claimed he had not known the police wanted to question him. The investigating officers were satisfied with his account of himself and sent him on his way with no further harassment. By this time the whole district of Whitechapel/Spitalfields had become volatile, the Ripper murders had hit local businesses hard, and people were so afraid to walk the streets after dark that shops and market stalls had been losing trade. Friends became suspicious and where once it was possible to go into any number of pubs and bars for a good drink and a friendly brawl, such violence was now viewed as a Ripper like activity. A normally united community was becoming divided as for the first time in London's history one man terrorized an entire community.

The local trades people of the district held an extraordinary meeting in an attempt to discuss and resolve the problem of diminishing trade. A petition was raised and submitted to the Home Secretary, Henry Matthews. This read:

> We the undersigned traders in Whitechapel, respectfully submit for your consideration the position in which we are placed in consequence of the recent murders in our district and its vicinity. For some years past we have painfully been aware that the protection afforded by the Police has not kept pace with the increase in population in Whitechapel. Acts of violence and of robbery have been committed in this neighbourhood almost with impunity, owing to the existing Police regulations and the insufficiency of the number of officers. The universal feeling

> prevalent in our midst is that the government no longer ensures the security of life and property in the East End of London and that in consequence of this, respectable people fear to go out shopping, thus depriving us of our means of livelihood. We confidentially appeal to your sense of justice, and ask that the Police in the district may be largely increased in order to remove the feeling of insecurity which is destroying the trade of Whitechapel.

Attached to this was a petition bearing the signatures of some two hundred trades people. The Home Secretary was unable to offer any immediate support to the petition and did not accept any personal responsibility. The Metropolitan Police had enough problems with the murders without having to become concerned and aware of personal security.

Sir Charles Warren's predicament worsened day by day. Aware that a number of individual agencies and authorities were attempting to hound him from office he trusted no one. Liaison with the Home Secretary was insignificant. Warren had made every possible attempt to apprehend the killer, flooding the district with high numbers of patrolling constables, the expense account had reached a critical limit with plain-clothes allowances taking up a high percentage of the figure. Somehow, despite all Warren's efforts, the killer had still managed to break through the police ranks and extract his seeming revenge on prostitutes. Warren believed the killer would make some error eventually, thus providing the police with vital evidence. Yet to provide such circumstances another crime would have to take place, another human life would be lost. The hunt became a personal vendetta for Warren, with victory to be sought at all costs. Charles Warren was unable to prevent himself from feeling a personal dislike to the miscreant who had caused his present predicament, but professionally he should not have become involved at a personal level with the crime he was investigating. Many astute members of Parliament recognized Warren's predicament and called for his resignation. Others, more vindictive, chose to address letters to the press which were derogatory and vicious. The press depicted Warren's difficulties with increasing enthusiasm, and every day which passed without another murder became a blessing to Warren for by now he was a broken man and almost ready to resign.

Mary Jeanette Kelly

Dorset Street (Duval Street) is situated deep in the heart of Spitalfields. In 1888 it was full of the worst type of criminals and other individuals imaginable. No more than two hundred yards in length it was crammed to capacity and a little bit more with the worst type of lodging-houses in the whole of the city. There were the odd few who could not afford to reside anywhere else than Dorset Street, but most people tried to get out of it as quickly as possible. In general, those who lived there had no money and no future, they had slipped through the fingers of time and into the depths of hell. Dorset Street was the centre for the beggar community and those who would attempt to steal or rob from people in the same void as themselves. Running westerly from Commercial Street and terminating at Crispin Street, Dorset Street was nothing more than a one-street slum. On one corner stood the Britannia public house. This pub, together with the Ten Bells and the Queen's Head on Commercial Street, was the central point of social activity. It was also the base for the thousands of prostitutes who wandered the streets.

One cool November morning (Friday the 9th), a local shopkeeper and landlord John McCarthy was busy in his shop in Dorset Street. McCarthy owned No. 26 Dorset Street, an awful slum which he had converted in a number of small rooms and leased out for a small sum, usually around 4s.6d. per week. Friday was rent day and McCarthy checked his files and noticed that the occupants of 13 Millers Court, 26 Dorset Street had not paid their rent and were in arrears to the sum of 29s. McCarthy told his assistant Thomas Bowyer to go round to the room and to demand some part payment against this debt, if nothing was forthcoming he was to threaten eviction. Bowyer left the shop and turned into a tiny alley which was around twenty feet long, this led into the small courtyard full of white-washed houses which was known as Millers Court. Bowyers walked along the alley whistling merrily to himself, eventually he reached the door of room No. 13 and knocked upon the rotting wooden panel. No reply was received and Bowyer repeated the exercise several more times before he walked into the court and peered through the filthy windows. He was reluctant to stare too hard into the room which he knew was occupied by a young Irish girl known as Mary Kelly who lived here with her lover called John or Joseph or some similar sounding name. Bowyer noticed that a window-pane was broken and tentatively placed his hand through the jagged glass and moved the old muslin curtain to one side. His eyes took a few moments to focus on anything within the damp dark room but when they did Bowyer felt his heart rate increase twofold. Blood covered the floor and the bed, a naked body lay upon the bed and its entrails were scattered about the room in various locations. The shocked Bowyer ran back to McCarthy and informed him of the find and both men ran to Commercial Street police station where they informed Inspector Beck of the facts. Within minutes the alert inspector and a few constables reached Millers Court. Beck peered through the broken window and gasped in horror at the sight before his eyes, at once he realized that it had to be another Ripper job. A telegram was sent to Scotland Yard and Superintendent Arnold and Inspector Abberline were dispatched accordingly. The area was sealed off and only authorized personnel were allowed to enter or leave Millers Court. News of the Ripper's latest atrocity spread through the community quickly and a large crowd assembled in Dorset Street screaming for the police to take action or to let the public hunt the man out. A near riot situation was imminent and the police did an excellent job in calming matters down.

Ninth November was the birthday of the Prince of Wales, rallies of celebratory gunfire could be heard echoing around the streets of Whitechapel and Spitalfields. It was also inauguration day for the new Lord Mayor of London, the Right Honourable James Whitehead. Dozens of streets were covered in bunting and banners to brighten up procedures for his parade as it passed along the route. Banquets and large dinners were organized for all social classes and it should have been a joyous occasion. The parade was almost complete when a buzz went around the crowd, news of the Jack the Ripper murder spread and suddenly a cacophony of newspaper boys cried out, 'Murder, Murder, loverly murder!' The crowds pushed and shoved to get the latest copies of the papers and read of the latest horrors in the East End. One policeman was bitten in the excitement and dozens of others hurt as the crowds fled into Whitechapel, leaving behind the pomp and circumstance of the Lord Mayor's parade. Within two hours, Commercial Street and other side streets running off the main thoroughfare were packed to the extreme. A constant throng of morbid sightseers flowed into the area in the hope of viewing some horrendous sight which they could relate to their families and friends. Without warning, a second buzz ran through the crowds. This time it was started by agitators who wished to remind everyone that it was one year to the day that the 'Bloody Sunday' riots had taken place in Trafalgar Square. The police were further attacked and suffered a heavy verbal barrage, but overall decency prevailed for the masses they were mourning the deaths of friends and neighbours not events of long ago. The police did a marvellous job in appeasing the crowd, but they could not hide the fact that after thirty-nine days rest Jack the Ripper was back.

On his arrival, Inspector Abberline requested that Sir Charles Warren's 'blessed' bloodhounds attend, although circumstances dictated that it would have been nigh on impossible for any dog to track someone down after the crowds had thronged the street thus destroying any possible scent. The police-officers on the scene had plenty of time to discuss their plan of action and were careful to leave the room exactly as it was. No one entered or even peered through the broken window other than Abberline and his colleagues. Various enquiries as to who occupied the room were made and it was soon confirmed that it belonged to Mary Jane Kelly. Abberline immediately instructed that her paramour Joseph Barnett be arrested and brought to Millers Court.

Unknown to any of the police-officers on the scene, Sir Charles Warren had resigned and both the bloodhounds had been returned to their owner in Scarborough. The divisional surgeon Doctor George Bagster Phillips arrived at the scene and viewed the carnage through the broken window and declared that there was nothing he could do for the person who lay dead upon the bed. All he could do was declare life extinct.

At 1.30 p.m., Superintendent Arnold made the bold decision to enter the sealed room and a whole window was removed allowing a photographer to climb inside and take valuable shots of the dead body *in situ*. After this operation was complete, the photographer left the room as he had entered since the main wooden entrance door was locked and the superintendent believed that by forcing it open vital evidence could be disturbed or destroyed. Curiously, the photographer took photographs of the victim's eyes in the belief that the retina retained the last image prior to death. With the preliminaries complete, John McCarthy was instructed to force open the entrance door using a pickaxe, allowing the officials to enter and view the horrors contained within.

The door swung open against a small bedside table to the right of the room. Beside it stood the bed with blood-saturated sheets and the mutilated corpse of the Ripper's latest victim. Various body organs which had been removed from the corpse by the killer had been laid upon the bedside table in a curiously neat fashion. All those who were present declared later that it was a scene which would live with them until their dying day. Neatly placed upon a chair on the opposite side of the room were the dead woman's clothes. Warm ashes were still present in the tiny fireplace and a man's pipe was found on the mantelpiece. A full search of the room was carried out resulting in significant minor finds; stale bread was found within an old cupboard and a number of ginger-beer bottles were also found, but little else which could be of assistance to the police. Two surgeons were tasked with picking up the body pieces and torso and placing them in bags to be taken to the mortuary. This took the best part of several hours and the battered coffin containing the dead woman passed along Dorset Street at 3.50 p.m. *en route* to Shoreditch mortuary. Once the body had been removed, the room was sealed and the windows boarded. A padlock and chain was used to secure the main door and a constable was positioned at the entrance to Millers Court. A more curious fact was the position of a poster offering a £100 reward for information leading to the Ripper's arrest, this was placed immediately opposite Mary Kelly's room. How the killer must have laughed as he read the poster, he knew only too well that he would never be caught by information received for he was a sole operator.

The body was identified at the scene by Joseph Barnett, Kelly's ex-lover. It was stated in at least one newspaper that he identified her by her ear, but I believe he may well have uttered hair and been misunderstood. Inspector Abberline was tasked with recording statements from all those who knew Mary Kelly and in making an inventory of all possessions found in 13 Millers Court. These included an engraving of the 'Fishermans Widow' which hung above the fireplace and an old broken wine-glass containing a burnt-out candle. Within the fireplace Abberline found various items of women's apparel including a hat and skirt, which had been all but destroyed by the fire. The spout of an old tin kettle had been melted off by some form of intense heat, but whether this is linked to the Millers Court murder or not is debatable. A simple explanation for the burnt clothing is that since it was a cold damp November evening, Mary Kelly wanted something to burn on the fire and chose a colleague's old clothing. There is something of a belief that the clothing had been placed upon the fire by the Ripper in an attempt to gain light. However as anyone who has ever attempted to burn old clothing will be aware, it does not ignite into a ball of flame but simply smoulders and smokes.

Within twenty-four hours of the murder, young boys were sighted on the streets of the district selling blood-red books entitled 'The Whitechapel Blood Book'. A fictional romanticized account of the murders, the colour of its cover added to the impression. The mood among the people of the area altered from depression to subdued apprehension, there was no end to this living hell and Jack the Ripper had become another problem of day-to-day life. Panic ran amok on the streets, violence between friends and neighbours reached crisis point and the whole environment was shrouded in gloom and despondency. Sunday 11 November saw the *Illustrated Police News* reveal:

> Great excitement was caused shortly before ten o'clock on Sunday night, in the East End, by the arrest of a man with a blackened face who publicly proclaimed himself to be 'Jack the Ripper'. This was at the corner of Wentworth Street, Commercial Street, near the scene of the latest crime. Two young men, one a discharged soldier seized him, and the crowd, which always on a Sunday night parade this neighbourhood, raised the cry of 'Lynch him'. Sticks were raised, and the man furiously attacked, and but for the timely arrival of the Police he would have been seriously injured. The Police took him to Leman Street police station. He refused to give any name, but asserted that he was a Doctor at St Georges hospital. His age is about thirty five years, height about five feet seven inches, complexion dark with dark moustache, and he was wearing spectacles. He wore no waistcoat but had an ordinary jersey beneath his coat. In his pocket he had a double peaked check cap, and at the time of his arrest he was bare headed. It took four Constables and two male civilians to take him to the Police station and to protect him from the

> infuriated crowds. He is deatained in custody and it seems that the Police attach great importance to the arrest, as the mans appearance answers to the description of the man wanted.

Typically the press exaggerated all events concerning the murders. At no time had the police issued a description of the wanted man as wearing spectacles and having a blackened face. The subject of this report was a lunatic and if press reports are to be believed then some weeks later this same individual was pulled out of the Thames having apparently committed suicide. Journalistic licence allowed varying arrests to be promoted into spectacular affairs.

There were the occasional press reports which seemed to depict the problems of the area quite accurately and adequately:

> The excitement in the neighbourhood of Dorset Street is intense, and some of the low women, with whom the streets abound appear to be more like fiends than human beings. The Police have naturally great trouble to preserve order, and one Constable who is alleged to have struck an onlooker was so mobbed and hooted by the crowd that he had to beat a retreat to Commercial Street police station, whither he was followed by a large crowd, who were only kept at bay by the presence of about half a dozen stalwart Constables who stood guard at the door preventing anyone from entering.

Whitechapel/Spitalfields it seems was as close as anywhere to a public riot, and it is difficult to understand just why further violence never erupted, especially towards the authorities. Even Queen Victoria became involved in the Whitechapel murders and in a personal memorandum to Henry Matthews she declared that the standard of detectives must be improved and that better lighting must be erected in the depressed areas. No one it seemed had any sympathy for the Metropolitan Police, not even Her Majesty.

With the sudden departure of Sir Charles Warren one could be forgiven for having some sympathy towards a police force whose leaders so often resigned in response to the fickle opinions of the public. Attitudes at Scotland Yard improved slightly and there were those who felt that the new commissioner James Monro would create a new force and one that could be reckoned with once confidence had been won back. Certainly the new commissioner had new ideas and implemented these in order to catch the notorious Whitechapel murderer. It was claimed that the Ripper was living on borrowed time! But, before long it became obvious that the new commissioner's ideas were little improvement upon those of his predecessor.

Monday 12 November 1888 saw the opening of the inquest into the death of Mary Jeanette Kelly. This was held at Shoreditch town hall and Doctor Roderick MacDonald was the coroner. The Metropolitan Police were represented by Inspector Nairn and Superintendent Arnold, with Inspector Abberline noticeable by his absence. The fifteen-man jury were sworn in and immediately asked why they had been chosen when the murder took place in another district. Doctor MacDonald retorted in a furious manner, 'Do you think that we do not know what we are doing here, and that we do not know our own districts? The jury are summoned in the normal way, and they have no business to object. If they persist in their objection I shall know how to deal with them. Does any juror persist in objecting?'

One juror had the confidence to reply, 'We are summoned from the Shoreditch district, this affair happened in Spitalfields.'

The coroner replied, 'I am not going to discuss this subject with the jurymen at all. If any juryman says he distinctly objects, let him say so. I may tell the jurymen that jurisdiction lies where the body lies, not where it was found, if there was any doubt as to the district where the body was found.'

Coroner MacDonald appears to have been an assertive official who did not suffer fools gladly, nor was he prepared to stand for animosity or ambiguity within his Court.

Eventually the inquest commenced and the jury were taken to the mortuary to view the final remains of Mary Jeanette Kelly, and to the murder site in Millers Court. With the preliminaries complete, Coroner MacDonald addressed members of the press:

> A great fuss has been made in some papers about jurisdiction and the Coroner and who should hold the inquest. I have not had any communication with Doctor Baxter upon this subject. The body is in my jurisdiction and was taken to my mortuary, and that was the end of it. There are no foundations for the reports that have appeared. In a previous case of murder, which occurred in my district, the body was carried to the nearest mortuary ... [in]

> another district. The inquest was held by Doctor Baxter, and to this I held no objection. The jurisdiction is where the body lay.

MacDonald had made his point and the press were forced to concede the matter as were the professional agitators who are present at all such public events. It is a great shame that the police could not be as authoritative in dictating the actual facts of the case to the press.

The first witness called to give evidence at the inquest was Joseph Barnett. The ex-boyfriend of Mary Kelly, Barnett had been arrested shortly after the discovery of the Millers Court affair. His was a familiar face to the Dorset Street community to whom he was known as Mary's husband. Barnett had been arrested along with dozens of other males during the police enquiry, as were all males residing in the district. However, none were as unfortunate as Barnett who now had first hand experience of losing a personal friend and lover, yet his display in the Court did not reveal any insight into Barnett's personal feelings about losing her.

> Barnett: I am a fish porter, and work as a labourer and fruit porter. Until Saturday last I lived at 24 New Street, Bishopsgate and have since stayed at my sister's, 21, Portpool Lane, Grays Inn Road. I have lived with the deceased for one year and eight months. Her name was Marie Jeanette Kelly with the French spelling described to me. Kelly was her maiden name. I have seen the body and identify it by the ear [probably hair. PH] and eyes, which are all that I can recognize, but I am positive it is the same woman. I lived with her in room number 13 Millers Court for eight months. I separated from her on 30 October 1888.
> Coroner: Why did you leave her?
> Barnett: Because she had a woman of bad character there, whom she took out of compassion, and I objected to it. That was the only reason. I left her on Tuesday between five and six p.m. I last saw her alive between half past seven and a quarter to eight on Thursday night last, when I called upon her. I stayed there for quarter of an hour.
> Coroner: Were you on good terms?
> Barnett: Yes, on friendly terms, but when we parted I told her I had no money and no work and had nothing to give her, for which I was very sorry.
> Coroner: Did you drink together?
> Barnett: No sir, she was quite sober.
> Coroner: Was she, generally speaking, of sober habits?

Barnett: When she was with me, I found her of sober habits, but she has been drunk several times.
Coroner: Was there anyone else there on Thursday night?
Barnett: Yes, a woman who lives in the court, she left first and I followed shortly after.
Coroner: Have you had conversation with the deceased about her parents?
Barnett: Yes, frequently. She said she was born in Limerick, and went when very young to Wales. She did not say how long she lived there, but she came to London four years ago. Her father's name was John Kelly, a gaffer or foreman in an ironworks in Caernarvonshire or Carmarthen. She said she had one sister who was very respectable, who travelled from market place to market place. This sister was very fond of her. There were six brothers living in London, and one was in the army. One of them was named Henry, I never saw the brothers to my knowledge. She said she was married when very young in Wales, to a collier named Davis or Davies, she said that she lived with him until he was killed in an explosion, but I cannot say how many years since that was. Her age I believe was sixteen, when she married. After her husband's death, she went to Cardiff to a cousins.
Coroner: Did she live there long?
Barnett: Yes, she was in the infirmary there for eight or nine months. She was following a bad life with her cousin, who was, I reckon and as I often told her, was the cause of her downfall.
Coroner: After she left Cardiff did she come direct to London?
Barnett: Yes, she was in a gay house in the West End, but in what part she did not say. A gentleman came there and asked her if she would go to France.
Coroner: Did she go to France?
Barnett: Yes, but she did not remain long, she said she did not like the part, but whether it was the part or the purpose I cannot say, she was not there more than a fortnight. She returned and went to Ratcliffe Highway, she must have lived there for some time. Afterwards she lived with a man opposite the Commercial gas works in Stepney. The man's name was Morganstone.
Coroner: Have you ever seen this man?
Barnett: Never, I don't know how long she lived with him.
Coroner: Was Morganstone the last man she lived with?
Barnett: I cannot answer that question, but she described a man named Joseph Fleming who came to Pennington Street a bad house where she stayed. I don't know when this was. She was very fond of him. He was a mason's plasterer and lodged in the Bethnal Green Road.

> Coroner: Was that all you knew of her history when you lived with her?
> Barnett: Yes, after she lived with Morganstone or Fleming I don't know which one was last, she lived with me.
> Coroner: Where did you pick her up first?
> Barnett: In Commercial Street, we then had a drink together and I made arrangements to see her the following day, a Saturday. On that day we both of us agreed that we should remain together. I took lodgings in George Street, Commercial Street where I was known. I lived with her until I left her on friendly terms.
> Coroner: Have you heard her speaking of being afraid of anyone?
> Barnett: Yes, several times, I bought newspapers and I read to her everything about the murders, which she asked me about.
> Coroner: Did she express fear of any one individual?
> Barnett: Our own quarrels were soon over, no sir.

At this point, Barnett was praised by Coroner MacDonald for his very respectable appearance which was unusual for one of his lowly class. MacDonald also praised the way in which Barnett gave his evidence, but closer scrutiny gives the impression that many of his answers were given in a staccato manner and were defensive rather than open. He seemed to deliberate over many replies and gave answers of no consequence to the inquiry, or which, at the very least, caused ambiguity.

The next witness called was Mary Cox of 5 Millers Court. She told how she had last seen Mary Kelly at a quarter to midnight when she was in an intoxicated state. Kelly entered Millers Court a few paces ahead of her in the company of a man whom she described as being short, stout and shabbily dressed wearing a long coat, his face was blotchy and he had a carrotty moustache, he carried a pot of ale in his hand. Mrs Cox had bid Mary goodnight and Kelly had replied, 'Goodnight, I am going to have a song'. Moments later Mary Cox heard the dulcet tones of Mary Kelly as she sang 'A violet I plucked from my mother's grave when a boy'.

During the following hours, Mary Cox came and went from her room on a number of occasions. She last heard Mary's voice at 1.00 a.m. and two hours later she claimed that she could see no light visible in Kelly's room. Cox had then remained within her room until 6.15 a.m. when she heard heavy footsteps walking from the court. This struck her as strange since it was too late for market workers to leave for work. Mary Cox further spoke of how she could normally hear the contents of any verbal arguments which took place within the court, and that she had heard nothing on the night of the murder. The coroner speculated that the footsteps might have been those of a patrolling policeman, but this idea appears to have been dismissed.

The next witness was Elizabeth Prater of 20 Millers Court, the room immediately above Mary Kelly's. Prater had returned to the court at around 1.20 a.m. on the morning concerned. Passing Mary Kelly's room, Prater claimed that no lights were visible and that the court was in total darkness. As she lay in her bed she awoke to a cry of 'Oh Murder', this was around 3.30 a.m. to 3.45 a.m. Prater dismissed the cry as a hoax, since it was a common enough call in this district. Eventually, at 5.00 a.m. she left Millers Court and once again passed Mary Kelly's room which was still in darkness. As she passed through the passage which led from the court and on to Dorset Street she noticed some men harnessing a horse, a common sight, and continued on her way to the Ten Bells public house in Commercial Street, totally unaware of the carnage which had taken place in the room directly beneath hers.

Sarah Lewis was visiting friends at 2 Millers Court on the morning of the crime. She too said she had heard a shout of 'Murder' at around 4.00 a.m. She further speculated that it was the cry of a female in distress, but due to the volatile situation within the East End had decided to ignore it.

Mrs Caroline Maxwell caused much confusion when she was called to give her evidence since it contradicted all that had been said before. Coroner MacDonald reminded Mrs Maxwell of the importance of telling the truth, but Maxwell insisted that what she said was the truth.

Maxwell claimed that she saw Mary Kelly around 8.00 a.m. and 8.30 a.m. on the Friday morning after her reported murder. Kelly was standing in the entrance to Millers Court which was opposite Mrs Maxwell's home at No. 14 Dorset Street. On seeing Kelly, Maxwell had said, 'What brings you up so early?', Kelly had replied, 'Oh Carrie, I do not feel so well', and Maxwell added that in her opinion Kelly did look quite ill. The astute coroner asked Maxwell why she knew Kelly's name when she had previously stated that they had only met twice before, but Mrs Maxwell explained that it took lodging-house people no time at all to get to know each other. Continuing, Mary Kelly had pointed out to Mrs Maxwell a pool of vomit which was in the street, she had been sick through over-indulgence in alcohol or, as she claimed, 'through drinking bad beer'. Maxwell said she had left Kelly in Dorset Street and returned at 9.00 a.m., when she believed she saw Mary standing outside the Britannia public house with a man with a moustache. The coroner once again intervened and instructed Mrs Maxwell to stand down from the witness box because of the ambiguous statements she was making. It may well be that Caroline Maxwell did not intentionally tell lies, but she was obviously confused by times and dates, and may have mistaken the events from a previous occasion.

Julia Venturney gave evidence of how she knew both Kelly and her paramour Joseph Barnett. She explained how Barnett would not allow Kelly to go out on the streets as a prostitute and he openly spoke of detesting her from acting in this way.

Maria Harvey of 3 New Court, Dorset Street, spoke of how she had slept in Mary Kelly's room on several occasions including the Monday and Tuesday evenings prior to Mary's death. Harvey said she had last seen Mary alive at 7.30 p.m. on the night of Thursday 8 November 1888, when she had been with Joseph Barnett in her room. Prior to his arrival, Harvey had been alone with Kelly, but she decided to leave when Barnett appeared. Harvey informed Kelly as she left that she would not return that evening but would call on her the following day. When she left, Kelly was alone with Barnett.

Doctor George Bagster Phillips took to the floor and was instructed by MacDonald not to release any information in relation to the actual extent of the injuries or to the ferocity of the attack. Abiding by these guidelines, Phillips informed the inquest that death had been caused by severance of the carotid artery. He refused to comment any further on the affair. It would seem that MacDonald's intention was to disperse the heavy media attention focused upon the Ripper killings. To his mind, if he were to prevent publication of the injuries sustained by the victim, then the press would have very little information to print about the crime. His attempt was in vain, as the press soon found an informant who provided the information they required to fill their pages. The injuries have been recorded as follows:

> The throat had been cut right across with a knife, almost severing the head from the body. The left arm, like the head, hung to the body by skin only. The nose had been cut off, the forehead skinned and the thighs down to the feet were completely devoid of any flesh. The abdomen had been ripped open and both breasts cut from the body. The liver and entrails had been torn from the abdomen, which in turn had been ripped across and down. The entrails and other portions of the body were missing from the remains, probably strewn around the room, but the liver and other such organs had been placed between the victim's feet. The flesh from the thighs and legs along with the breasts and nose, had been placed upon the bedside table in an attempt by the murderer to display his artistic talent. The left hand of the victim had been pushed deep into the gaping abdomen. It was also believed that the woman was three months pregnant, but the foetus was missing.

It has generally been accepted that the Ripper took away all of the missing organs, but this has never been proved, and it is more likely that he destroyed them by burning them on the fire, or cutting them into such tiny pieces that it was impossible for the authorities to identify them. It is not reasonable to assume that after committing this horrific crime he took away with him various parts of the anatomy. He would have no need for such items and to do so would have increased the likelihood of his capture.

Inspector Abberline was the next witness called to give evidence and he found himself answering basic questions upon the police enquiry and clearing up any ambiguities which had arisen during the hearing. Coroner MacDonald asked Abberline whether the door to Kelly's room was locked and, if so, how the murderer had made his escape? Abberline replied, 'An impression has gone abroad that the murderer took away the key of the room. Barnett has since informed me that it has been missing for some time, and since it has been lost they have put their hands through a broken window and moved back the catch, it is quite easy.' If it was so easy, then why was this action not carried out by the police or Barnett while photographs of the dead woman were being taken. Why did John McCarthy have to force the door open using a pickaxe? A complete window and frame was removed from the room so that the photographer could gain entry to take his photographs. Surely, once he was

The Ten Bells, Commercial Street. A popular pub frequented by Liz Stride and, indeed, all the victims and their killer . . .

hristchurch, Spitalfields.
he local parish church

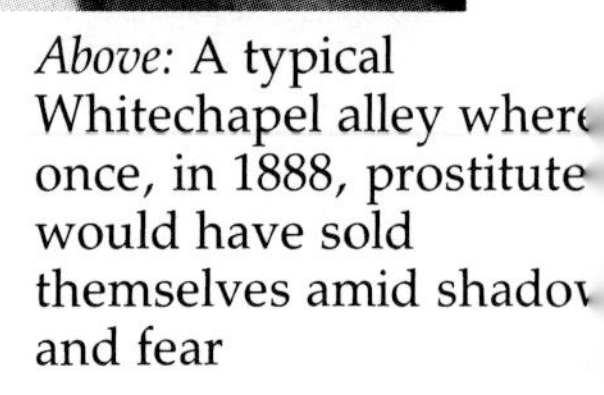

Above: A typical Whitechapel alley wher once, in 1888, prostitute would have sold themselves amid shadov and fear

Left: Two sketches of the supposed murderer released the time of the inquiries

'Ripper's Corner' in Mitre Square today where over a century ago Catharine Eddowes met her death

Another view of 'Ripper's Corner' showing the City of London boundaries

The rear of Wentworth Dwellings, Goulston Street

The notorious doorway where Jack the Ripper is supposed to have scrawled a message concerning the 'Juwes' and where he left a piece of Catharine Eddowes' apron covered in faecal matter. Sadly the doorway has long since been demolished within the room he would have been instructed to open the door using the catch which must have been visible to all who viewed the room since it was only two feet or so from the broken window. I find it impossible to believe that enquiring police-officers would not have looked at a way to enter the room. It must be said that the catch was not the method used to secure the door on this occasion, there is too much evidence to the contrary, therefore it must have been locked using the mortice lock and key. Yet Barnett claimed that the key was missing, and had been lost. It is not conceivable that the Ripper could have found a key and instinctively known which door it would fit, unless that is he was known to his victim and could remove the key without anyone else knowing what he had done. At last we have some evidence linking the Ripper to a victim. Abberline also told of the contents of Kelly's room, including the man's clay pipe, which he nonchalantly passed off as belonging to Joseph Barnett. There were no questions as to why Barnett had left it there.

Abberline stood down and MacDonald took centre stage. He rambled on about his duties and responsibilities as a coroner and more or less forced the jury into returning a verdict of 'Wilful murder by some person or persons unknown'. All this in just one day. With his task complete MacDonald officially closed the inquest into the mysterious death of Mary Jane Kelly.

MacDonald's lack of enthusiasm means that many questions remain unanswered. The information available on this crime is further complicated by evidence which came to light after the inquest. George Hutchinson, an unemployed labourer, reported to Commercial Street police station at 6.00 p.m. on Monday 12 November 1888, and made the following statement:

> About 2.00 a.m., 9th, I was coming by Thrawl Street, Commercial Street, and just before I got to Flower and Dean Street, I met the murdered woman Kelly, and she said to me, 'Hutchinson, will you lend me sixpence?', I said 'I can't I have spent all my money going to Romford', she said, 'Good morning, I must go and find some money'. She went towards Thrawl Street, a man coming in the opposite direction to Kelly tapped her on the shoulder and said something to her, they both burst out laughing. I heard her say 'Alright' to him, and the man said, 'You will be alright for what I have told you', then he placed his right hand around her shoulders, he also had some kind of parcel in his left hand, with a

> kind of strap around it. I stood against a lamp of the Queen's Head public house and watched him, they both came past me and the man held down his head, with his hat over his eyes. I stooped down and looked at him in the face. He looked at me stern. They both went into Dorset Street, I followed them, they both stood at the corner of the court for about three minutes. He said something to her, she said, 'Alright my dear come along you will be comfortable'. He then placed his arm on her shoulder and gave her a kiss. She said she had lost her handkerchief, he then pulled his handkerchief, a red one out and gave it to her. They both then went up the court together, I then went to the court to see if I could see them but I could not, I stood there for about three quarters of an hour to see if they came out, they did not so I went away.
>
> Description: age about thirty four or five, height five foot six inches, complexion pale, dark eyes and lashes, slight moustache curled up each end, and dark hair. Very surley looking, dress long dark coat, collars and cuffs trimmed astracan, and a dark felt hat turned down in the middle. Button boots and gators with white buttons, wore a very thick gold chain, white linen collar, black tie with horse shoe pin, respectable in appearance. Walked very sharp, jewish appearance can be identified.

This is perhaps one of the most remarkable witness statements I have ever read. The description and attention to detail are inspirational and never, in eleven years of practical police work, was I fortunate enough to record such a statement of witness from an individual. Sadly, Hutchinson's eye for detail destroys the credibility of the statement. The notion that Hutchinson could have seen the man's eyelashes is ridiculous, especially when one takes into account the lighting conditions, the shade thrown from the brim of the man's hat, and shadows from facial features. My suspicions are aroused by the statement that the man was carrying a parcel in his left hand. How very convenient! The press had revealed that the police believed the killer to be left-handed, and here is an archetypal description of Jack the Ripper complete with parcel in his left hand supposedly containing his knives. Finally, if Hutchinson was so suspicious of this individual, why did he not report it to the police at the time or come forward before the closure of the official inquest? Hutchinson's man is a figment of his imagination. The character is straight from the stage of a music-hall and the details are too precise to be true. No one would be stupid enough to walk around that area at that time of morning dressed as Hutchinson's man was. A man of affluent appearance would run the risk of mugging and robbery or even murder. Hutchinson's statement has no bearing upon the Ripper enquiry. George Hutchinson was an average Victorian Londoner who wished to make a name for himself. He retold his story to dozens of reporters from various newspapers and depending upon their fees would reveal more or less detail.

Hutchinson was interviewed by Inspector Abberline on a number of occasions and each time he repeated the identical description as though he had been programmed to repeat nothing else. The authorities humoured Hutchinson but refused to comment on the matter to the press. Abberline appears to have refuted all claims that this was a description of the man wanted, but he let it be known that he wished to speak with the man described by Hutchinson as soon as possible in order to eliminate him from the enquiries. The supposed description of Hutchinson's man was published on the front pages of some newspapers, and it is a perfect description of a child's view of a mad killer, right down to the mad staring eyes complete with thick bushy eyebrows. There is a rather weak theory that the police intentionally delayed the release of Hutchinson's statement as they did not wish it to be heard at the inquest. This is pure supposition. The date in ink inked at the top of Hutchinson's statement clearly states 12 November 1888, and it is more likely that the police would have preferred Hutchinson's statement to be read at the inquest since it would have assisted their attempt to gain some credibility.

Monday 19 November 1888 saw the church bells of St Leonard's, Shoreditch, ringing loud and clear. The clanging acted as a magnet for thousands of people who slowly gathered at the church. The funeral of Mary Jane Kelly was seen as a community event. The fact that Jack the Ripper had had the audacity to enter an East End home and commit his horrendous deeds was taken as a personal insult by many locals who felt as if they had been exposed and raped by this mysterious villain who walked their streets. As Mary Kelly's coffin appeared from within the church, the crowd sobbed and moaned in unison, personal friends wept openly and it seemed that a whole community wished to grieve the prostitute's death. The coffin was placed onto an open-backed cart and dozens of outstretched arms and hands attempted to touch it. Upon the polished elm coffin lid lay two artificial crowns of flowers and a cross of heartsease. These had been donated by friends and customers of the Britannia and Ten Bells public houses. Two other carts containing official mourners escorted the coffin. Initially there were problems in getting the cortège moving through the dense crowds, but with a smart policeman at hand it got under way. At last the cortège arrived at the gates of St Patrick's Roman Catholic cemetery, Leytonstone. The mourners were met by Father Columban who was accompanied by two acolytes and a cross-bearer. The coffin was taken from the cart and into the north-eastern corner of the graveyard. As the coffin was lowered into the ground, Joseph Barnett displayed much emotion and knelt upon the wet grass and sobbed. The crowds stood in silence respecting the passing of one of their kind, and eventually some fifteen minutes later everyone began to drift away. Two planks were placed over the grave along with the two wreaths which served as a temporary memorial of the last resting-place of Mary Kelly. An interesting tale concerns the scene after the crowds had drifted from the cemetery and was first told on national television in 1959, in a programme titled 'Farson's Guide to the British' which was hosted by Daniel Farson. Apparently, a woman who was visiting another grave in the cemetery on the day of Kelly's funeral was paying her last respects to her bereaved when she noticed everyone leaving the Kelly grave – everyone that is except one man who obviously believed he was alone in the area, parted the planks and spat upon Mary Kelly's coffin. An interesting tale, but I am dubious about its accuracy. Still, it displays just how much myth has been created from simple events pertaining to the Ripper killings.

All expenses incurred in Mary Kelly's funeral were met by Henry Wilton, the sexton of St Leonard's Church. Wilton claimed that his actions were in response to the feelings aroused by the community who were unable to raise sufficient money to provide a decent burial. At first it was proposed that a headstone should be erected from public funds, but insufficient funds were collected and the idea was soon forgotten. For over one hundred years the grave remained unmarked. It is only in recent times that a headstone has been erected to remind people who lay in the densely populated space beneath it, crowded with bodies and coffins, and by whose hand she had met her untimely death.

We are told that the official Ripper inquiry ended after the Millers Court murder since the crimes of Jack the Ripper then ceased. Some say that the killer committed suicide since his brain gave way after the awful glut in Millers Court. Others that the killer was incarcerated in a lunatic asylum, others even claim that the Police knew the identity of the man they wanted but, as he was in a lunatic asylum they felt it to be in the best interests of his relatives not to divulge his identity. Like so many other myths connected with the Ripper, these suggestions are nonsense. The police were desperate to locate and apprehend the killer. Having suffered greatly at the hands of the press and public, they wanted to reverse the humiliation which had been brought upon them and would hardly have suppressed such information. Many police-officers of the time recorded their disappointment at not catching the Ripper in their respective memoirs. Subsequently, amateur detectives attempted to reveal the existence of a secret guild among police-officers who had pencilled marginalia in their memoirs so that the case could be solved at a later time. The inference is that the police knew who the Ripper was and chose not to reveal his identity publicly. Now this may be so, but why they should choose to suppress this information is difficult to understand and I cannot see such reasoning holding much credence with the authorities. It is certain that documents were received by Scotland Yard in 1888 and much of what was received was genuine, but the marginalia within Robert Anderson's autobiography – although original – can in no way be classed as vital evidence which reveals the real identity of Jack the Ripper. The fact of the matter is that Jack the Ripper was never caught and the case remains unsolved. Despite various attempts no one, until now, has been able to link the killer with the victims, or even supply a decent motive. Theories have been complicated and unreasonable, but in reality everything has a reasonable solution, once one identifies the evidence leading to it.

In 1888, the police were under great pressure from the press, public and politicians alike, even Her Majesty the Queen denounced the activities of the detective service, and they were pressured into making on the spot decisions.

Unlike present-day criminologists and Ripperologists, the police of 1888 did not have the luxury of time and research material. The officers directly involved in the case were not permitted to make decisions, but received instructions from the Ivory Towers of Scotland Yard as to who was an ideal suspect and who was not. This blinkered vision prevented patrolling officers from following up enquiries on the local populace. Today's criminologists are all too keen to point out errors in police enquiries and rulings, but policing then was in its infancy and even now a killer such as Jack the Ripper would be difficult to locate, especially with the number of clues available, which in Victorian Jack's day were non-existent. The police were used as pawns by the press and public and were not to blame for the majority of errors which have been credited to them. I do feel that the police were given a rough ride during this particular enquiry, and undoubtedly the bad press hindered enquiries and ultimately allowed the Ripper to escape detection.

Over the years which followed 1888, a number of murders were closely linked with the crimes of Jack the Ripper, especially those committed in the same district. Some were officially recorded within the Ripper file, others have been linked by the press in an attempt to maintain interest in a story which sells copies. Officially, the police file on the Whitechapel murders remained open until 1892, but nothing sinister should be read into this, other than the fact that police-officers were still regularly involved in continuing enquiries within the district. By 1892, it was obviously felt that the individual whom the police suspected had stopped killing or had absconded. Certainly, by that date, they felt sure that no further Ripper crimes were being carried out. His appetite satiated, he had lost the need to kill.

3 Copy-cat Attacks

Before venturing any deeper into the world of myth and legend surrounding the various Ripper suspects, I feel that the 'Copy-cat' attacks which took place around the same period should be discussed and examined. Some of these took place prior to the five murders ascribed to the Ripper. Various attempts have been made to connect these crimes with those of the Whitechapel murderer, but to date no firm evidence exists which permits such a claim to be authentic.

It is now an accepted fact that in any serious criminal investigation other crimes of a similar nature will occur, but without the distinct trademarks which identify a particular individual. The crimes of Jack the Ripper were simulated by various people within months of the Millers Court tragedy, some of the culprits were arrested and punished, others escaped. Nineteenth-century London was volatile, particularly the East End with its different religious and political factions. During the 1880s murder was a common cry in Whitechapel/ Spitalfields and even in neighbouring Bethnal Green. Prostitute murder was by far and away the most common crime of violence. Murders were usually committed with a knife, normally it was a straightforward stabbing or throat-cutting. However policemen who came across bodies with cut throats could not discount suicide as a remarkable number of people commit suicide by cutting their own throats. It was the horrendous mutilations Jack the Ripper carried out which thrust his crimes into the public eye and captured the imagination of the press. A naîve Victorian society could not comprehend how one human being could perform such atrocities upon another living person. With the advent of the Ripper crimes, the press seized every opportunity to promote murder in the East End, hence other murders have been drawn into the legend, to which they are in fact in no way connected. It is worthwhile examining these crimes and disproving this mythical connection.

In March 1888, Ada Wilson sat in the living-room of her tiny home at 19 Maidman Street, when a man suddenly forced his way in and demanded money with menaces. Ada Wilson was shocked by the sudden attack, but refused to hand over anything of material value. Her enraged attacker stabbed her twice in the throat and ran away empty-handed. Fortunately, Ada Wilson survived the attack and was able to provide the police with a full description of her assailant: aged thirty years with a sunburnt face and a fair moustache. He wore a wide-awake hat, and was five feet six inches tall. This description is not dissimilar to the later descriptions of the Ripper. However, it seems incredible that anyone could believe the Ripper would force his way into someone's home and demand money for robbery played no part in the Ripper crimes. Hence this attack must be considered an opportunist crime by some individual requiring material gain.

Easter Monday 3 April 1888, saw Emma Elizabeth Smith, a 45-year-old prostitute and mother of two young children, being followed by a group of four men as she patrolled her regular patch touting for business. The men eventually stopped Smith in Osborn Street and physically abused her, forcing some kind of blunt instrument into her vagina tearing the perineum. The attack complete, they fled from the scene and were never seen again. Emma Smith somehow managed to stagger to her lodgings in George Street, Spitalfields. On arrival there, she collapsed and explained what had occurred to her lodging-house keeper. Amazingly Smith then summoned enough strength to stagger round to the London Hospital on Whitechapel Road where the full extent of her injuries was revealed. She had suffered serious internal injuries and was bleeding profusely from her vagina, in order to stem the flow of blood she had stuffed a rag between her legs. The police were notified of the attack and raced to the hospital where they interviewed the by now confused Emma Smith. The woman was able to describe her attackers in some detail, but soon drifted into an unconscious state and died. Despite various police enquiries, no one was ever brought to justice.

The Ripper was a sole operator and not part of a gang. Emma Smith may have been the victim of a spasmodic attack by one of the local gangs who lived off prostitutes' immoral earnings. The attackers were unlikely to be apprehended as they would provide each other with alibis.

In the early hours of Tuesday 7 August 1888 a prostitute by the name of Martha Turner/Tabram was found brutally murdered on the first-floor landing of George Yard buildings. She had been savagely attacked with a sharp-bladed instrument. Her body suffered thirty-nine independent stab wounds, seven of which were in the lungs, six in the stomach and one in the heart, the rest covered the torso and in particular the area surrounding the vagina.

The police commenced enquiries and soon confirmed that the victim had been out with another prostitute by the name of 'Pearly Poll' on the night of her death. 'Pearly Poll' was traced and informed the authorities that they had met two Grenadier Guards and had eventually left each other alone with their respective partners. Despite numerous identity parades, she was unable to identify positively the two men whose company they had been in that fateful night. To this day the crime remains unsolved, though the Grenadier Guard theory seems highly probable since the wounds inflicted upon the body of Martha Turner/Tabram were like those caused by a bayonet.

Many crimes remained unsolved in this district, but this particular murder attracted much media attention and whipped up much local animosity towards the police. As far as Jack the Ripper is concerned, this particular crime was most influential in the development of the myth, but the particular traits of the Ripper are once again absent, the carotid artery was not cut, the body was not mutilated. However, like the Ripper, the killer had some grievance against prostitutes since it takes much strength to stab someone thirty-nine times.

Just twelve days had elapsed after the dreadful murder of Mary Kelly in Millers Court when another Ripper scare was launched upon an unsuspecting public. Annie Farmer, a 40-year-old prostitute, had spent a long cold night on the streets of Spitalfields. It was around 7.30 a.m. on Tuesday 21 November 1888 when she met a man who was familiar to her, not by name but by sight. He was an ex-client and it was some time since they had last met. After getting over the customary preliminaries, the man suggested that they share a bed at Satchells lodgings, 19 George Street. The bed cost 8d. which was paid by the man. According to Farmer, the couple were in bed when suddenly the man lunged at her throat and tried to cut it. Instinctively she screamed, 'Murder, murder'. On this, the man fled the lodgings and disappeared into the cool morning air. Farmer ran into the kitchen of the lodging-house and showed her injury to the housekeeper who sent for the police. Within minutes, the police arrived on the scene and interviewed Farmer. It was obvious that she did not require medical attention as the wounds to the neck proved to be no more than a reddening which could have been caused by an irritation. There was something about Farmer's attitude which caused the police to disbelieve her story in its entirety. Soon the woman had told detectives that the attack was provoked over an argument about money, (possibly payment by the man or the theft of money by Farmer). A sharp-eyed detective noticed that Farmer spoke with an odd tone and asked her what was in her mouth. Though she denied having anything in her mouth, she was then forced to open it and a number of coins dropped on to a table. The event was a farce, but the police expressed concern over the attack and wished to locate the attacker urgently. Meanwhile, the press arrived at their own conclusions and named the man as Jack the Ripper. One paper confidently announced that the 'Ripper was back'. The police soon revealed information which proved that the attack was not in any way similar to the previous attacks committed by the so-called Whitechapel murderer.

The next attack came at 4.15 a.m. on Thursday 20 December 1888 when Police Constable Robert Goulding found the body of Rose Mylett in the rear yard of 184–186 Poplar High Street. The body was in a typical Ripper pose, on its back with the legs drawn up. The only thing which was absent was any form of physical assault. Once again the press hammered home the suggestion that this was another Ripper-orientated crime. Doctor Phillips, the divisional surgeon, was called to the scene and asked to examine the body. He confidently declared that death had been caused by strangulation as shown by tiny marks on the neck. In front of enthusiastic reporters, Phillips added that the Ripper had strangled at least one of his victims and had known just where to place a ligature for maximum effect as in the case he had just examined. The police were furious at Phillips' unethical outburst and at once denied any association between this attack and previous Ripper attacks. It was decided that a second opinion should be called in and the police requested that Doctor Thomas Bond of Westminster should examine the body. Bond was well respected by the upper echelons of London for his sensible approach and calming influence over somewhat inexperienced doctors. After his examination, Bond declared that there was no evidence of strangulation, no marks on the neck nor the facial disfigurement or bruising which tended to accompany a strangulation attack. He further claimed that on the morning of her death, Rose Mylett had been incapacitated through over-indulgence in alcohol, she had fallen over in a drunken stupor and choked to death on the collar of her coat. Prior to the inquest, Coroner Baxter was informed of these facts, but amazingly he elected to believe the inaccurate version supplied by Doctor Phillips. Baxter stated that of the five surgeons who had examined the body, only Bond had found no evidence of strangulation, and because of this he forced the jury to return a verdict of murder. Despite this, the police refused to accept this decision and opted to accept Doctor Bond's opinion which was based on a post-mortem carried out much more methodically than those of the other doctors.

The comments of Doctor Phillips were just what the press had ordered. With artistic journalistic licence they attempted to make much of the mysterious death of Rose Mylett. But, for once, the police refused to budge from their initial opinion, with a united front they successfully overcame the challenge of the press and the case of Rose Mylett returned to obscurity.

This was the final panic of 1888. The horrors of the year began to slip from memory, as the whole community returned to normal life. For seven months the legend of Jack the Ripper echoed round the streets and alleys of the East End, but people could not believe that he was gone, his needs satisfied or fulfilled.

Terror returned in July 1889 when another murder was committed and this time all of Jack's trademarks were evident.

Police Constable Andrews walked slowly along Castle Alley.

It was approaching 1.00 a.m. and his duty sergeant had just left him, having carried out his customary supervisory visit. It was 17 July and Andrews' mind was probably full of thoughts about his refreshment break and where he could scrounge a mug of steaming hot tea. As he weaved through the maze of empty coster-barrows Andrews paused. He saw a form lying beneath one of the barrows and tentatively he approached it. To his surprise it was the remains of a woman, her throat had been cut and much of her clothing disarranged. The constable blew hard on his police whistle. He believed he had found another Ripper murder. The duty sergeant returned to Andrews and asked what the problem was. On viewing the body, he too felt it was a Ripper murder. After a short time Doctor Phillips arrived and officially reported that, 'The woman's neck was incised on left side with wound jagged'. Further examination revealed abdominal injuries. The wounds inflicted were not deep enough to open the cavity, but varying degrees of abrasions were clearly evident. At the resulting post-mortem Doctor Phillips, who was assisted by Doctor Brown, recorded that bruising found on the victim's chest was caused by the attacker kneeling on the chest whilst cutting the throat. He added that he had worked on each of the bodies of the Whitechapel victims and as such he was qualified to state that this particular job was not connected. The severence of the throat on this occasion had been caused by a short-bladed knife, not the six-inch one used by the Ripper. Sir Robert Anderson requested a second opinion from Doctor Bond, who was to find the body in the early stages of decomposition thus making it more difficult to ascertain precise causes of marks. In a memorandum to Anderson, Bond states:

> I see in this murder evidence of similar design to the former Whitechapel murders viz, sudden onslaught on the prostrate woman, the throat skilfully and resolutely cut with subsequent mutilation. Each mutilation indicating sexual thoughts and a desire to mutilate the abdomen and sexual regions. I am of the opinion that the murder was committed by the same person who performed the former series of Whitechapel murders.

In order to refresh the public's minds the press recalled the Ripper's previous work and attempted to instil panic in the city. However, they failed since Jack the Ripper was old news and the police now had a much more professional image and appeared to be winning over the public as they cleared the streets of criminals. As well as this, a greater scandal hit the news that July concerning an alleged brothel in Cleveland Street involving young boys and many influential and high-powered men. Interest died once the police announced the identity of the victim in Castle Alley as 'Clay Pipe' Alice MacKenzie. This crime remains unsolved, but it is possibly connected with a pimp who had a grievance against Alice.

The next panic took place in the early hours of 13 February 1891 when police constable Ernest Thompson found the body of a woman lying in the road near Chamber Street. Her throat had been cut and Thompson believed that he might have disturbed the killer since he heard someone running from the scene. Remaining with the body, Thompson blew his police whistle for assistance. That he never thought of following his fleeing suspect may be put down to his inexperience since he had only been in the job for six weeks or so. A constable on an adjoining beat heard the shrill tones of the police whistle and rushed to his colleague's aid. Constable Ben Leeson arrived at the railway arch which spanned Royal Mint Street and Chamber Street to see Thompson standing there with two men, who were in fact local night-watchmen. Thompson informed Leeson of the facts of his find and further told his colleague that it was another Ripper job! A quick inspection of the body by the more experienced officer soon explained just why Thompson had reached this conclusion. Apart from a great gash in her throat, the woman had sustained abdominal injuries. Leeson recognized the woman as 'Carrotty Nell' Frances Coles, a local prostitute. He further found her to be still alive but it seemed obvious that she would not survive for any length of time. Coles was taken to Leman Street police station where she was examined by Doctor Phillips who pronounced life extinct.

Enquiries led police to a description of the man wanted. He had been to Coles' lodging-house on the night of the murder, one of his hands was bleeding and he had explained to the lodging-house keeper that he had been the victim of a mugging during which he was beaten and robbed. The housekeeper refused to allow him access and turned him away, only for him to return a short time after and be once again refused access. Presently a man was arrested in Whitechapel and taken to

Leman Street police station. The news spread and there was much rejoicing in the streets for some police-officers had alerted the public that the Ripper had at last been caught. Various police officials visited the station during the hours which followed gave rise to further speculation that it was the Ripper who had been caught. This was confirmed when Chief Inspector Donald Swanson, at one time head of the Ripper enquiry, arrived and later departed in an apparently jocular frame of mind.

The arrested man was James Saddler, a drunken fireman from the SS *Fez*. He had been heard to threaten Frances Coles with her life and seemed a logical suspect. The crowds in Leman Street became agitated as news from within the police station died down. Unknown to them, Saddler had been taken via the rear of the station to Holloway Prison (which did not become a women's prison until 1902), more for his own safety than anything else. The ship's fireman requested the assistance of the National Seamen's Union, who gladly jumped at the opportunity to defend one of their own. Such a powerful defence was built around Saddler that the law courts had no alternative but to find him 'Not guilty'. The police had by this time ascertained that Saddler was too drunk to be capable of committing such a crime and was therefore innocent. To this day, the crime remains unsolved.

The Frances Coles murder was the last such crime to be linked with Jack the Ripper. It was claimed that certain authorities on the matter had stated that the Ripper had drowned in the Thames, or had been committed to a lunatic asylum. No one could agree upon his fate, but what is certain is that when James Saddler was arrested the police did believe they had captured the Ripper. Nothing else could explain why so many senior police officials attended Leman Street police station to view and question a simple murderer. The action of these top officials in attending the tiny police station reveals that they thought the Ripper was alive and well and still operating in 1891. The fact of the matter is that the police had no clue as to the identity of Jack the Ripper dead or committed. A few may well have had their suspicions, but proving these was another matter.

Of all the officers who claimed to know the true identity of Jack the Ripper only one, in my opinion, would have had any authority to make such a claim, and that one officer elected not to record his memoirs thereby leaving his opinions open to discussion. It is alleged that Abberline claimed the Ripper was a Russian feldsher known in England as George Chapman. Yet, in a *Pall Mall Gazette* in 1903, Inspector Frederick Abberline is reported to have made the following statement: 'You must believe we have never believed all those stories about Jack the Ripper being dead, or he was a lunatic or anything of that kind'. Abberline, though, was simply hedging his bets. He knew that it was impossible for him to speak his mind for if it could be proved that the Ripper had been someone other than George Chapman, he could be sued for defamation of character. The fact that he chose not to write a book on his police service career speaks much of the man, for Abberline probably knew Whitechapel/Spitalfields better than any other detective involved in the Ripper enquiry. Although he would not admit it, saying that the Ripper enquiry was just one of many and was no more special than the others, Abberline resented the fact that the Ripper escaped justice.

By 1892, Abberline had been removed from the Ripper enquiry and younger more inexperienced detectives were allowed to review the case. This in itself has created major problems for latter-day Ripperologists, since these inexperienced officers went on to record their memoirs and give the false impression that they were actively involved in the Ripper enquiry and had inside information on the case. From their conclusions come the dozens of theories and myths which have been created over the one hundred years or so since the murders. Ask any police-officer his honest opinion of the majority of the theories proposed and most would reply that the solutions proposed are far too complicated. The Whitechapel murders have become shrouded in a veil of mystery and theorizing which in reality does not exist.

Continuing with the search for the identity of the killer and the truth behind the Jack the Ripper legend, I will examine each suspect and the various types of criminal in an attempt to glean some kind of evidence which could help us establish who is the illustrious criminal known as Jack the Ripper.

4 The Chosen Few

The actual number of people who over the years have been suspected of being Jack the Ripper number around thirty including a trained ape and the devil himself.

Personally, I thought one of the most humorous solutions was that the Ripper was a reincarnation of Renwick Williams (The Monster) who was arrested by the authorities in the late eighteenth century for stabbing women in the backside with a small pocket-knife. Williams was a fetishist who was regularly caught committing such minor offences. He was hanged for his crimes in 1790, and his elevation to the position of Ripper suspect was brought about by foolish talk in the East End's gin palaces and pubs in 1888 and later. It is human nature for one person to pretend to know something no one else does, hence the number of rumours circulating about Jack the Ripper. A further mystery is why the legend endures.

The amount of literature available on the crimes of Jack the Ripper is enormous, with books, magazines and complete newspaper articles devoted to the case. Almost all such publications profess to reveal new evidence. Sadly very few live up to their reputation. The one factor absent from almost all previously proposed theories is evidence. Fact cannot be denied. Though the amount of hard evidence available after a century is limited, circumstantial evidence can be as damning as real evidence and many murderers have been punished on such evidence. In this chapter I intend to consider the case for and against each of the various suspects and assess the facts with a professional's eye. It will soon become apparent to the reader that the accusations directed at many of the high profile suspects are based upon fictional events. Cases against other suspects are plausible and well researched, but lack that vital factor called evidence.

I hope to prove to you that Jack the Ripper can have been none other than the suspect I have researched for six years, a man who was suspected by the police of the time.

Montague John Druitt

Born: 15 August 1857.
Occupation: Barrister/School-teacher.
Died: December 1888.

Over the last two decades this individual has proved to be the most popular suspect ever named or proposed. This is mainly due to dramatic statements made by Sir Melville MacNaghton, assistant head of CID, and which are included in the Scotland Yard files. The notes, which are known as the MacNaghton papers state:

> A Mr M.J. Druitt, said to be a Doctor and of good family, who disappeared at the time of the Millers Court murder, and whose body (which was said to have been upwards of a month in the water) was found in the Thames on 31 December 1888, or about seven weeks after that murder. He was sexually insane and from private info I have little doubt that his own family believed him to have been the murderer.

Startling stuff, but first let us look at Druitt's life in the years up to 1888.

Montague John Druitt was born in Wimborne, Dorset, his father was a leading surgeon and a Justice of the Peace. After spending six years at Winchester School, he won a scholarship to New College, Oxford. Unfortunately, he never equalled his aspirations and in 1878 just managed to obtain a second-class honours degree in Classical Moderations. Druitt graduated in 1880, and applied for admission to the Inner Temple sometime in May 1882. With the confidence of a good schooling behind him, Druitt believed he could be a proficient barrister, but found to his cost that it was an expensive occupation; to subsidize it, he took up a teaching post at Blackheath Private Boys School. Within one year he was called to the bar, and to maintain a good impression took shares in chambers at 9 King's Bench Walk, London. He joined the Western Circuit and the Winchester sessions, but found the going hard and never managed to obtain a full brief.

Maintaining his interest in teaching, Druitt was enthusiastic about his work at Blackheath School until November 1888 when he was mysteriously dismissed. No official reason for this has ever been forthcoming, but it has been spuriously suggested that he had homosexual tendencies. This is, of course, pure speculation since there is not one scrap of evidence to confirm this.

Montague Druitt was last seen alive on 3 December 1888. His body was found floating in the Thames near Thorneycroft Torpedo Works, Chiswick on the last day of December 1888. His coat pockets were full of heavy stones.

This, believe it or not, is the basis for the claim that Montague Druitt was Jack the Ripper. The 'evidence' against him comes in a variety of forms. It is claimed that his mother, who had been confined to a mental institution in 1888, had a great influence on him as he believed that he was insane through a hereditary disease. However, although the precise location of the Brooke Asylum is not known today, it is believed that it was almost two miles from Whitechapel. Accompanying this is the claim that the chambers at 9 King's Bench Walk were the ideal base for his Ripper operations, being less than a mile from Whitechapel or Spitalfields. Furthermore, his cousin Lionel Druitt was a doctor and had served as a locum in the Minories in 1879. It is claimed that Montague may have been a regular visitor to the surgery where he could watch his cousin operating and gain some anatomical knowledge. Through his visits to the Minories and to his sick mother, he gained a thorough geographical knowledge of the East End. And finally there are stories of a pamphlet existing in Australia titled *The East End Murderer, I knew Him* by Lionel Druitt. While it is certain that Lionel Druitt emigrated to Australia, there is no record of such a booklet.

Further research into Druitt by Irving Rosenwater (*The Cricketer*, January 1973) revealed that he was a first-class cricketer and an all-round sportsman, playing regular cricket for many top-class clubs in the south of England. This suggests that Druitt was strong and physically fit, attributes which the Ripper was deemed to possess.

We have a marvellous biography of Montague Druitt's life, but absolutely no evidence concerning the violence or sexual insanity claimed by MacNaghton. They do not exist. There is no real link between Druitt and the East End. The conclusions drawn from the fact that his cousin Lionel lived and worked in the Minories are very weak. The Minories are hardly part of Whitechapel/Spitalfields and, in any case, Lionel only lived at 140 the Minories for a short time. He is listed in the *Medical Directory* as practising there in 1879, and the following year lists him as practising at 8 Strathmore Gardens – hardly sufficient time for Montague to get to know the area. It has been proved that Lionel emigrated from his address in Strathmore Gardens, so he never actually practised in the Minories again. Even if Montague visited his cousin in the Minories, it does not prove he was the Ripper! That Druitt used his room in King's Bench Walk as a base for his Ripper operations is totally contrary to the available evidence. After the Mitre Square murder the killer headed north along Goulston Street and on to Dorset Street. King's Bench Walk is to the south of Mitre Square, and there is no reason why Druitt should head in totally the opposite direction towards territory where he would run the risk of being beaten or mugged.

Further evidence against Druitt being our man comes from documented records of cricket matches. On the morning of Annie Chapman's murder, Druitt was in Wimborne in Dorset playing cricket. It is highly unlikely that he killed a prostitute at 5.30 a.m. and then continued on his way to Wimborne to play first class cricket, all within a few hours.

Many criminologists and official authorities have searched for the booklet in Australia, but no one has ever heard of it or seen it. The whole case against Druitt is built upon hypotheses and innuendos.

The question is, therefore, why should a senior police official mention Druitt in the files? Closer scrutiny of the document suddenly reveals discrepancies in MacNaghton's claims, his conclusions become contradictory and clearly incorrect as far as the case against Druitt is concerned. When Druitt's body was fished from the Thames, it would have been police policy to search his residence for evidence as to why he had committed suicide and the police would have been especially certain to do this if he was a Ripper suspect. During the search, which must have taken place, the police would have located evidence which tended to prove that Druitt was the Ripper. Such evidence could not have been kept secret in the police force and someone would surely have let a piece of information slip. Under no circumstances would the police have withheld the name of the Ripper from courtesy.

Sir Melville MacNaghton was never actively involved in the Ripper enquiry, yet, in his official notes, he claims that 'from private info' he believed Druitt to have been the Ripper. It is most unlikely that MacNaghton would have kept this 'private info' to himself and deliberately broken regulations.

MacNaghton gives the false impression that he knows all the facts of the case. However, he makes mistakes, for example, he claims Druitt was a doctor when in fact he was a barrister – how can one mistake the two? In his biography, *Days of my Years*, MacNaghton states: 'I incline to the belief that the individual who held up London in terror, resided with his own people, that he absconded himself from home at certain times, and that he committed suicide on or about 10 November 1888'. This cannot possibly be Montague Druitt who did not reside with his own people and who was last seen alive on 3 December 1888.

MacNaghton's speculations destroy the fine research into Druitt's life carried out by many authors. However, since there is no positive evidence to link Druitt to Whitechapel, or to violence, or to a motive, we must conclude that Montague John Druitt is a scapegoat, and totally innocent of all that he is accused. Perhaps his ghost may now be finally laid to rest!

George Chapman alias Severin Antoniovich Klosowski

Born: 14 December 1865.
Occupation: Barber/Surgeon and publican.
Died: 7 April 1903.

Born in Nargonak, Poland, Severin Klosowski appears to be the one individual who holds the key to the Ripper saga. He was the favourite suspect of Inspector Abberline.

In his native country, Klosowski served as an assistant surgeon in Praga. He later joined the Russian army as a feldcher or barber/surgeon. In 1881 he was employed as an apprentice to a surgeon in Zvolen town. After serving this five-year apprenticeship, he attained his junior surgeon's certificate and moved to Warsaw where he struck up a close friendship with a hairdresser's traveller known as Wolff Levisohn.

In 1888 Klosowski moved to London where he worked as a barber's assistant in Whitechapel High Street. A shadowy vague character, the records of his exact whereabouts are difficult to locate, but some time in 1889 he resurfaced as the owner of a barber's shop in Tottenham High Street. In the same year he went through a bogus marriage ceremony with a Polish woman called Lucy Baderski. The couple lived in Cable Street, Whitechapel. It was not long before Klosowski's real wife arrived in Whitechapel from Poland but after a brief stay with her husband and his pseudo-wife she returned to Poland. The barber's shop failed, so in late 1889 Klosowski and his sham wife left England in search of a new life in Jersey City, America. Once in America the couple set up another shop, which was successful for a short time, but Klosowski changed in his new environment, he suddenly became a womanizer and in consequence Lucy Baderski returned to England in February 1891 with their two children. 1892 saw Klosowski return to Lucy and family but the relationship was not the same and the couple parted the following year.

Severin Klosowski was not slow where women were concerned. In the same year, 1893, he took up residence with another woman known as Annie Chapman (no relation to the Ripper victim). Once again the relationship was anything but steady and Annie decided to leave her lover. It was this relationship which caused Klosowski to alter his name to George Chapman and to drop his true identity.

Within weeks, Chapman had met with Mary Isabella Spink, a 41-year-old divorcee. Chapman trapped the woman with his charm, persuaded her to marry him, and a bigamous marriage ceremony took place. Chapman was able to get his new partner to finance the purchase of a barber's shop in Hastings but, like everything else Chapman touched, it failed. The couple returned to London after purchasing The Prince of Wales, a public house off the City Road. For a short time life seemed to improve and Mrs Spink respected her hard-working partner who was, unknown to her, planning her death. On 2 April 1897 Chapman purchased one ounce of tartar-emetic poison from a local chemist, which was issued against receipt of signature.

One ounce of this poison is sufficient to kill up to ten people. Before long Mrs Spink became ill and Chapman hired a neighbour to nurse her, while he maintained business in the pub. Chapman insisted on cooking all Isabella's meals himself, a fact which struck the neighbour as strange but one which she never questioned. On Christmas Day 1897 Mrs Spink died, the cause of her death was officially recorded as phthisis. The following day, Chapman opened the pub as usual.

Chapman's immediate concern was to employ further female bar staff to assist him in the running of the bar. He soon found a willing volunteer in 33-year-old farmer's daughter, Bessie Taylor. Within months, the couple went through Chapman's typical bogus wedding ceremony and, like her predecessor, Bessie soon began to feel unwell. For some reason the couple left the Prince of Wales and moved to the Grapes in Bishop's Stortford. Bessie soon found that her possessive partner had a violent streak, on one occasion he actually threatened her with a loaded revolver. Bishop's Stortford did not suit either of the couple, so it was decided to move back to London where they took over the Monument Tavern in Union Street. Bessie Taylor's health continued to be a source of concern and she died on 13 February 1901. Chapman was now a double murderer who had escaped all suspicion. Each of the medical experts who examined the body of Bessie Taylor came to a different conclusion as to the actual cause of her death, such incompetence is rare in the medical service.

In August 1901 Chapman fraudulently married 19-year-old Maud Marsh who was very much under the influence of her parents. Indeed, Maud's mother harboured a deep mistrust of Chapman founded on the mysterious death of his previous wife. It did not take long for Maud Marsh to fall ill, but her mother intervened as soon as this occurred and nursed her back to health, refusing to allow Chapman to interfere.

With murder in mind, Chapman moved pubs yet again, to take over the Crown in the same street. It was a busier pub with the chance of more money. It was also smaller in living accommodation to make it difficult for Mrs Marsh to stay overnight. Maud fell ill again and this time her mother decided to make her suspicions known. She informed her own doctor and requested that he examine Maud and find out if she was being poisoned. The doctor did as he was asked and came to the same conclusion as Mrs Marsh – someone was deliberately poisoning Maud. The doctor contacted Maud's personal physician, Dr Stoker, and informed him of the facts, requesting that the situation be monitored. Sadly, before any further action could be taken, Chapman had administered the final fatal dose and Maud had died. Doctor Stoker refused to sign the death certificate until a post-mortem had been carried out. This infuriated Chapman who called the doctor incompetent and tried to convince the practitioner that his wife had died of natural causes. His claims fell upon deaf ears. A private autopsy was carried out and revealed traces of poison in the body. Without further ado, Chapman's previous two wives were exhumed and further traces of poison were found in their remains.

George Chapman was arrested for murder on 25 October 1902. It is claimed that when Inspector George Godley advised the then Chief Inspector Abberline of the arrest the latter said, 'So you have caught Jack the Ripper at last.' George Chapman's trial lasted just four days and the jury took only eleven minutes to find him guilty. He was hanged at Wandsworth Prison on 7 April 1903.

Could George Chapman have been Jack the Ripper? He could have been, but the evidence relies very heavily upon other people's comments. The statement allegedly made by Abberline when answering George Godley who had informed him of Chapman's arrest is only part of a sentence. We need to know its context and how accurate George Godley recalled it. In any case, such hearsay evidence is of no use in any criminal trial and Abberline's comments cannot be construed as an accurate picture of his innermost feelings.

Doctor Thomas Dutton, an eminent criminologist of the era and a personal friend claimed Abberline had assisted him in compiling *Chronicles of Crime,* a collection of records of individual crimes. Dutton claims that Abberline was in a barber's shop in Whitechapel when he overheard someone say 'Ludwig'. Abberline, it is claimed, had recently interviewed a suspect of the same name and he suddenly realized that the two men were actually one and the same. Abberline became highly suspicious of 'Ludwig' and decided to interview him again, but on his return to the barber's shop he was told that 'Ludwig' had left. He was told that the man's surname was something like

'Shloski'. Dutton claimed this was a mispronunciation of Klosowski! Abberline eventually traced his man, but could find no further evidence to warrant making an arrest so George Chapman alias Severin Klosowski remained free.

Dutton claimed that when Chapman/Klosowski was in Jersey City, similar Ripper crimes took place there, and on his return to England they ceased. He said that Abberline interviewed Chapman's/Klosowski's original wife, who informed him that her estranged husband maintained very strange hours often returning home between 3.30 a.m. and 4.00 a.m. She could give no excuse for these absences and felt suspicious of him. Finally, Dutton claimed that the Ripper correspondence contained certain Americanisms such as 'Dear Boss', which he felt was natural slang Chapman would have picked up in America.

This then is the case for George Chapman being Jack the Ripper. Is it true or false? First, the Ripper-style murders which took place in Jersey City while Chapman was over there do not exist. It is a total fabrication of the truth. The famous *Chronicles of Crime* compiled by Doctor Thomas Dutton have mysteriously disappeared and only a few people claim to have seen them prior to their disappearance. Those who have seen them are united in the opinion that they were full of incorrect data. For example, the legendary writing on the wall in Goulston Street which Dutton claimed to have photographed and retained copies of the negatives. In the *Chronicles of Crime* Dutton misspells the word 'Juwes'. Some, indeed, are of the opinion that the *Chronicles* may not actually exist.

Perhaps, though, the most telling argument is the fact that no serial murderer has ever successfully altered his murder technique. There is a great divide between poison and physical violence. Jack the Ripper was an exhibitionist who wanted public acclaim. It is not possible that overnight he should suddenly shun fame in favour of the anonymity of poison – the coward's weapon. A mutilator has a completely different personality to a poisoner. The mutilator is physically involved in a violent murder and enjoys the feeling of complete control over his suffering victim. A poisoner prefers to slink away and imagine the pain his victim is going through without actually letting the victim know who or what is destroying him. The manner of death is very different, poison victims die a slow, laborious and often painful death, the victim of a violent crime dies quickly though a great deal more destructively.

Finally, if George Chapman had been the notorious murderer of the five Whitechapel prostitutes, then it has to be said that he would want the credit for his actions and might have confessed in the condemned cell. More curiously, it seems that Godley, who claimed that Abberline believed Chapman was the Ripper, never once questioned him about the matter. We are left with nothing more than pipe-dreams. Abberline's belief that Chapman was the Ripper was misplaced, the quotes of Godley and Dutton are incomplete and inaccurate, and George Chapman was not Jack the Ripper.

Thomas Neill Cream

Born: 27 May 1850.
Occupation: Doctor.
Died: 15 November 1892.

Born in Glasgow, Scotland, Thomas Neill Cream was the eldest of eight brothers and sisters. At the age of thirteen he moved with his family to Montreal, Canada. While there he often taught at Sunday school and seemed to be an ideal young man. Soon he enrolled as a medical student at McGill University and qualified as a doctor in March 1876. It is without doubt that Cream had a promising career in medicine ahead of him, but for some inexplicable reason he embarked upon a life of crime which led to his death. His first offence was committed whilst he was at university when he apparently set fire to his lodgings in Mansfield Street. This he carried out with malice aforethought since he had recently insured the premises. The insurance company were alert to such trickery and refused to pay out a full claim, and a compromise was agreed at $500.

Doctor Cream then found that a relationship which he had been having with a girl by the name of Flora Brooks had hit a snag, the girl was pregnant. Cream persuaded the girl to let him carry out an illegal abortion. He did this, but her parents realized what was going on and at gunpoint forced Cream to marry Flora. The honeymoon lasted just one day, and Cream left Canada *en route* to England where he arrived in October 1876. It was not long before he enrolled as a post-graduate student at St

Thomas's Hospital, but soon after he returned to Canada with the news that his wife had died. Cream promised his in-laws that he would never see them again if they paid him $200.00, which they did.

Cream then set up an illegal abortion business, with blackmail thrown in as a sideline. His reputation as a fraudster became so notorious that he was forced to move to Ontario, Canada. While there he was arrested for the murder of Kate Gardener, a patient of his who had died after one of his unprofessional abortions. However, this slippery character wriggled out of the charge and was officially cleared in a court-of-law. His reputation was so infamous, that he was forced to leave Canada for America where he set up business in Chicago. Although his business there was legitimate, two patients died of his mishandling of drugs and treatment. He also entered into a relationship with Mrs Stott whose epileptic husband sent her to Cream's clinic to collect his medication. Over the weeks which followed, the couple led an active sex life and Mrs Stott regularly spoke of how she wished she could be rid of her husband. Cream decided to play God, poisoned her husband, and persuaded Mrs Stott to run away with him.

For reasons best known to himself, Cream decided to write to the coroner of Boone County and advise him that Stott's death was the fault of the chemist who had added too much strychnine to the medication. Cream also requested that the body be exhumed and a full autopsy be carried out. This was done and it revealed that Stott had died as a result of poisoning. Cream was arrested and jailed for second-degree murder. He was sentenced to serve his punishment in Joilet Prison, Illinois as prisoner 4374.

Cream procured his release in July 1891 having served less than two years for the crime for which he was punished. He returned to Canada and then to London, where he arrived that October. Taking up residence in Lambeth, Cream was generous with his sexual favours towards women. He soon spent occasional nights with a 26-year-old prostitute by the name of Matilda Clover, and within two weeks of his arrival in London he had embarked upon a poisoning spree. The first to go was a 19-year-old prostitute called Ellen Donworth (Linnel) who was found writhing in agony in the Waterloo Road. Before her death she described a man who had given her some pills to aid her complexion. It was Cream. Next on the list was Matilda Clover, she too was found rolling in agony and died before any further information could be gleaned from her. The doctor who carried out the final examination of her body gave as the cause of her death, 'Natural Causes'!

Cream was not satisfied with escaping punishment for his crimes. Boastfully he sent various missives to the authorities blaming certain individuals for the death of Matilda Clover. He used a pseudonym when writing such letters. As well as taunting the authorities, he sent a letter demanding £2,500 to a doctor whom he blamed as the cause of her death, or at the very least, Cream claimed, the doctor had failed to recognize symptoms which could have been treated to save the woman. The letter was handed to the police who retained it. Not yet satisfied, Cream wrote next to the coroner informing him that Ellen Donworth had also died by poison. He asked for a mere £300 to reveal the required information. Once again, the letter was handed to the police who noted the handwriting was similar. For some reason Cream never followed up his blackmail threats, and it seems that the letters were sent in order to tease the authorities and to show how clever he was, in much the same way as Jack the Ripper.

For a short time, Cream refrained from his criminal activities and fell sincerely in love with a woman called Laura Sabbatini. In early 1892 they became engaged to be married. Cream left his new love for a short time, returning to some unfinished business in Canada. While there he had 500 leaflets printed informing readers that any person eating at the Metropole Hotel was in danger, as the poisoner of Ellen Donworth was now in the employment of the hotel. The leaflets were never distributed, but give a brief insight into Cream's frame of mind at that time, he was obviously deranged and unable to maintain his hitherto unsuspecting manner. Eventually, he returned to England on 2 April 1892 where he settled into London life with a three-in-a-bed romp with two prostitutes, Alice Marsh and Emma Shrivell. The two women were to be his next victims for shortly after he left them they were found dead. However, Cream had been sighted by an observant policeman who was aroused by his furtive actions as he left the house.

Cream resumed his literary campaign by accusing a doctor's son of the murder of the two prostitutes and asked for £1,500 to remain silent on the matter. Once again the letter was handed to the police, who this time were able to trace the writing as that of Doctor Thomas Neill Cream. The doctor remained at liberty until he made his most foolish error. He began to ramble on about the various murders in the district to all who would listen and even took people on guided tours of the murder sites, revealing an in-depth knowledge of the crimes. At last, he took a local acquaintance around the sites and spoke of how the killer had committed his crimes and escaped justice; the mistake Cream made was that his latest acquaintance was an off-duty police sergeant named McIntyre. The end came when Cream was recognized by the policeman who had sighted him leaving the home of the two murdered prostitutes. Cream was arrested on 3 June 1892 and tried and found guilty of murder. On 15 November 1892, Cream ascended the scaffold at Newgate Prison where the executioner, James Billington positioned him and placed the hood over his head. Standing back, Billington drew back the trap-door bolt and as he did so Cream is alleged to have said, 'I am Jack the …' the sentence was never completed, Thomas Neill Cream was dead.

We are now encroaching on to comic-strip stuff where the killer reveals his true identity at the moment of death – all very dramatic, but incorrect. Cream may well have fancied himself as Jack the Ripper but he could never have escaped detection with his silly letters and notes to the authorities pointing out his sins. It is without doubt that he was a poisoner of immense evil but, like George Chapman, he could not have been the Ripper because a serial murderer who uses poison does not then turn to violent mutilation.

In addition, there is documentary evidence which proves that he was incarcerated in Joilet Prison during the Ripper's reign of terror in Whitechapel. To accept the Cream theory, one must have a very great imagination. The records dictate that Cream was jailed during the ten weeks of terror in 1888.

It is claimed that the legendary KC Sir Edward Marshall Hall once defended Cream on a bigamy charge. Cream's defence was that he was imprisoned in Australia at the time of the offence. Sure enough, the governor of the prison confirmed that someone of Cream's description was in his jail during that period and all charges against Cream were dropped. Are we to believe that for the purpose of the Ripper crimes Cream had a double who would serve as an alibi as and when required? Cream's bravado on the gallows is to be admired when for the first time in his life he displayed courage, but Neill Cream was no Ripper.

Frederick Bayley Deeming

Born: 1842.
Occupation: Various.
Died: 23 May 1892.

For many years a death mask on view in Scotland Yard's Black Museum was referred to as that of Jack the Ripper. It was in fact that of Frederick Bayley Deeming, a mass murderer of the late nineteenth century.

Deeming was born on Merseyside in 1842, the youngest of seven children he was very much attached to his mother's apron-strings. For many years both his parents sheltered him from the real world, providing him with financial assistance even though he was more than capable of earning his way through full-time employment. In 1860 he obtained employment as a ship's-steward and travelled the world in the course of this job. Every so often he returned to Merseyside with fantastic tales of wealth and women. Occasionally he would have a blue-eyed, raven-haired beauty on his arm. In 1873, the mother he so adored died. Deeming became emotionally disturbed by this tragic event and refused to forget her, mourning continually for a considerable time after the event.

Eventually he resumed his seafaring adventures. During one such voyage he suffered a severe attack of brain fever, from which it was claimed he never recovered. Every so often he would commit some ludicrous act and infer that his dead mother had instructed him to do it. Somewhere on his travels Deeming met and married an English woman, and four children were born of this relationship. In 1887 while in Australia he was arraigned on a bankruptcy charged and jailed for fourteen days. It seems that fraud was his particular forte since he was regularly questioned by Australian detectives dealing with such matters. With his responsibilities Deeming decided that a family move would be of benefit to all, so in 1888 the family moved to

Capetown, South Africe where Deeming earned the reputation of a cheat and a bad debtor and was forced to move again, this time to Johannesburg, where he resumed his petty crime activities.

With all this harassment, Deeming decided to send his wife and family back to England, to Merseyside. After committing further petty crimes, Deeming too returned to England. After a brief spell on Merseyside with his family, it became obvious that Mrs Deeming and the family had disappeared. Deeming countered suspicion by explaining that they had gone away. After a while he could stand no more and returned to Australia where he remarried and moved to Melbourne. Shortly after, the new Mrs Deeming disappeared and Deeming told friends and neighbours that she had gone away on business. Deeming left the house in around Christmas 1891. The house stood empty until March 1892 when the owner escorted a prospective renter around. The woman asked what the repugnant smell was in the dining-room. The owner could offer no immediate explanation, but on speaking with neighbours it was recalled how the previous occupant's wife had mysteriously disappeared. The police were notified and the dining-room floor lifted to reveal the remains of Deeming's second wife. Her throat had been cut. The Australian police contacted their English counterparts and asked them to be on the look out for Deeming. The police went to Liverpool where Deeming owned a cottage. Neighbours told officers that his family had disappeared almost overnight. The floor to the kitchen of his English home was lifted and there the police found the bodies of Deeming's first wife and four children. All had sustained horrific throat injuries which had caused death.

In March 1892, Deeming was arrested in Perth, Western Australia. During the subsequent journey from Perth to Melbourne, Deeming appeared to suffer some form of fit, kicking and thrashing all over for about one hour before he finally appeared to come to his senses. It was believed by some that he was attempting to feign insanity, but the fit did little for his apparent quest for public sympathy, indeed it had the opposite effect as he was ridiculed for it.

The pre-trial publicity was enormous. Some newspapers stated that Deeming had been sighted in Whitechapel in 1888, others professed to have seen him purchasing knives in

Death of Kelly

Forcing open the door of 13 Millers Court to reveal untold horrors within

low: 13 Millers Court, orset Street. Once the venest of Mary Jeanette elly and Joseph Barnett, d the scene of her otesque murder

Below: An official police photograph of Mary Jane Kelly after the Ripper had finished with her. Breasts and other organs have been laid on the table beside her, and her left hand has been thrust by the killer into the cavity of her stomach

Joseph Barnett in court. The 'friend' of the deceased

Billingsgate fishmarket restorec to its former glory. Here Barnett studied his trade . . .

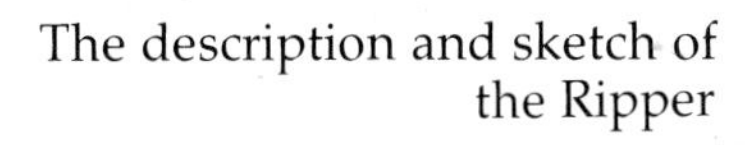

The description and sketch of the Ripper

The sketch that the press issued

Joseph Barnett, from a contemporary sketch

In this very row of houses Jack the Ripper, better known to his neighbours as old Joseph Barnett, died unaccused

How it all ended

Inspector Abberline's retirement home in Bournemouth

Whitechapel shops. The implication was clear, the press wanted Deeming to be the Ripper. It was claimed that whilst in prison Deeming had told fellow inmates that he was Jack the Ripper, but failed on each occasion to confess to the police authorities. During the trial, Deeming claimed that he suffered from epileptic fits and brain disease caused through contracting venereal disease whilst at sea some years earlier. Deeming claimed this was what caused him to kill. He also claimed that the pre-trial publicity had been against him and had declared him guilty before he was tried. It was a moving speech and perhaps caused a brief flutter in the hearts of the jury, but he sealed his own fate when he declared that the people present in the court were among the ugliest race of people he had ever seen. Such comments hardly endeared Deeming to the jury or the public. The jury took just over one hour to find him guilty of murder. The death penalty was passed and, despite various attempts by his family to appeal against the sentence, he was hanged on Monday 23 May 1892. The last view his fellow inmates had of him was as he calmly strolled to the gallows puffing on a huge cigar.

The reasoning that Deeming was the Ripper stems from enthusiastic journalists who were on the look out for a scapegoat. Certainly the motive of insanity caused through venereal disease, presumably from a prostitute, is quite good; but the fact that Deeming was in jail in South Africa at the time of the murders must be conclusive. Like Neill Cream, Deeming could not have been the Ripper since he was in another country at the time.

HRH Prince Albert Victor, Duke of Clarence

Born: 8 January 1864.
Died: 14 January 1892.

The claim that Jack the Ripper was related to the highest in the land has been a popular myth since 1970. Can there really be a more scandalous theory? This speculative theory received mass media attention, but though it seemed at the time that the claim was valid, the facts do not link together.

His Royal Highness, Prince Albert Victor, Duke of Clarence

and Avondale was the grandson of Queen Victoria and the eldest son of the future King Edward VII. Had Clarence lived long enough he would eventually have become king. However, he was robbed of his birthright by pneumonia which killed him in January 1892, thus allowing his younger brother George to claim the title.

November 1970 saw the first story break concerning Clarence and the Ripper. It was released upon an unsuspecting world in the *Criminologist* in an article by Doctor Thomas Stowell CBE MD. Stowell was a retired surgeon who claimed to have examined the private and personal papers of Sir William Gull, who at one time had been Physician Extraordinary to Queen Victoria. Stowell claimed that he had stumbled across the information by accident and explained that while Gull referred in the papers to Clarence as the Ripper he was careful never to actually mention his name. However, there was no doubt in Stowell's mind that this was the true story of Jack the Ripper.

In 1879, Clarence and his younger brother embarked upon a three-year world cruise, on board the HMS *Bacchante*. The Royal cruise visited Australia and while there it is claimed that Clarence was seduced. It further transpires that from the sexual encounter Clarence contracted syphilis which causes softening of the brain. Another consideration is that Clarence had not yet recovered from an attack of typhoid and in consequence his young body was unable to fight the vicious disease.

On return to England, the prince led a frail and timid life, stumbling from one illness to another. After a time, he began to lead an alternative life in the bistros and taverns of various suburbs of London, behaving like a commoner. 1889 saw the infamous Cleveland Street scandal break into the news. It was claimed that the young prince had become involved in homosexuality. There were stories of boys receiving golden pencils in part payment for the sexual delectation of high society. The scandal became known as the 'Golden Pencil' enquiry. Stowell states that the scandal became such an acute embarrassment to the Queen and the Government that the prince's equerry fled the country and Clarence was packed off to sea until the investigation was over. It is further postulated that Sir William Gull, who also acted as Clarence's personal physician, had declared that Clarence was educationally subnormal and that Queen Victoria was concerned about this especially as he was in line to the throne.

On 4 January 1892, Clarence attended the funeral of Prince Victor of Honenloe in London. It was a bitterly cold day and the unsuspecting Clarence, who had suffered from a heavy cold for most of the preceding month, caught another infection and became seriously weakened. When, a short while after, the Royal family assembled at Sandringham to celebrate the young prince's birthday, the majority were suffering from colds and sniffles caused by a particularly bad flu epidemic which had spread across the country. In London, where Prince Victor's funeral took place, this was worsened by dense damp fog which had descended around Christmas time and had refused to lift. On 7 January, the day before his birthday, Clarence was out shooting in the grounds of Sandringham, when he fell ill again. He was carried back to the house and put to bed where he remained, his condition deteriorating by the hour. Finally, on 14 January 1892, the heir presumptive passed away.

Stowell claimed that the recorded cause of death was false and believed that Clarence had died as a result of venereal disease which had softened his brain and led him to commit the Ripper murders. Stowell claimed that the Royal family would be forced to deny the allegations since to admit that one of their own number had been the Ripper would rock the roots of society and destroy England's heritage.

The Gull papers are now missing and Stowell has no evidence to prove his case. He makes a great play on words. I know of no one, apart from Stowell, who claims to have seen the Gull papers.

I have many objections to this theory, the principal one being that Clarence was officially reported as away from London at the time of at least two of the crimes. The morning after the double murder he was reported as being present in a hunting-party at Balmoral, Scotland. When Mary Kelly was murdered, he was at Sandringham celebrating his father's birthday. There is of course a remote chance that he could have slipped away from such activities and returned to London, but it would have been an awfully tight schedule. Neither is it reasonable to suppose that he could have left the Royal household without the staff or family noticing his absence. The prince had no knowledge of Whitechapel or surrounding districts and Stowell does not explain how he travelled to and from the area. Furthermore, if the prince's health failed after he contracted syphilis, how could he have committed the atrocities in Whitechapel since the Ripper was a fit young man in good health and not a weak constituted misfit with a weak constitution.

Stowell's theory is ingenious, but inaccurate and presumptuous. There is no evidence available, other than statements which Stowell alleges appear made in papers now missing and the fact that Clarence died young.

He may well have possessed certain papers owned by Sir William Gull, but certainly nothing that would incriminate royalty. Gull's judgement was good and had the Royal family any suspicion that his papers accused one of their number of being the Ripper they would have been destroyed before any outsider read them. Stowell died shortly after his revelations were released, on the eighty-second anniversary of Mary Kelly's murder, it seems that the pressures brought on by mass media attention were all too great for him to bear. To his credit Stowell never actually named Clarence, he referred to him throughout as the mysterious 'S'. The first man to publicly name Clarence as the Ripper was Kenneth Allsop, a journalist who interviewed Stowell on BBC TV – although Stowell denied the allegation. In print, Clarence was first named by Colin Wilson in an article in the *Leicester Chronicle* in 1973; Wilson said Stowell had told him 'S' was Clarence some years previously. In his biography of Clarence, Michael Harrison dismisses this allegation.

There is no possibility that Clarence could have been Jack the Ripper. There is no evidence, only an ambiguous claim. I confess I find it disturbing that anyone should want to believe Royalty could commit such distressing acts.

James Kenneth Stephen

Born: Unknown.
Occupation: College tutor.
Died: 3 February 1892.

It seems that anyone who died during this era runs the risk of being labelled a Ripper suspect. This particular theory again involves Royalty, albeit to a lesser degree, and it is based upon Doctor Thomas Stowell's theory and the real identity of his mysterious 'S'.

James Kenneth Stephen was the son of the famous 'Mad Judge' Sir James Fitzjames Stephen who had earned his nickname from his somewhat erratic behaviour during the trial of Florence Maybrick in 1889 who was tried for the alleged murder of her husband through poisoning. Stephen's summing-up of the case was more than a little biased, forcing the jury to return a guilty verdict. Spectators in the court abused Stephen verbally with cries of incompetence. At a later date, the death penalty was revoked by the Home Secretary who deemed that Mrs Maybrick should be jailed rather than executed. Sir James' crass incompetence proved to be a deciding factor in his removal from the judicial circuit.

The young James Stephen knew little of his father's fall. He studied hard at Eton and later at Cambridge University. An intelligent young man, he developed a great interest in poetry and the basics of the English language, and eventually gained an excellent name for himself as a part-time tutor. Such was his fame among the social élite that he was approached by the Royal family who requested that he act as personal tutor to Clarence. It is speculated that during such tutorials a homosexual relationship developed between the two young men, and that Stephen gained a hold over Clarence, guiding him towards certain political beliefs.

In 1884 Stephen was called to the bar. He desperately wanted to emulate his father in the legal profession, but like so many others he failed to obtain a brief. The relationship with Clarence continued, until the prince was forced to leave university to continue with his Royal appointments. In consequence, his relationship with James Stephen diminished and according to the theory, James Stephen became insanely jealous of the young prince and his preference for different friends.

In 1886, James Stephen received serious head injuries in a horse-riding accident in Suffolk. He was taken to a London hospital where he was examined by none other than Sir William Gull, who prescribed a strict course of medication to remedy the problem. It is claimed that Stephen failed to recover from the injury and became mentally unstable. He felt confused and betrayed in his relationship with Clarence, and decided to commit various murders in order to embarrass the Royal family. Stephen embarked upon the Whitechapel murders which were committed on certain 'Royal' anniversaries. The theory then relates to ten separate murders:

Emma Smith	3/4 April 1888	Feast of Cybele
Martha Turner	6/7 August 1888	Duke of Edinburgh's birthday
Polly Nichols	31 August 1888	Princess Wilhelmina's birthday
Annie Chapman	8 September 1888	No anniversary recorded
Liz Stride/ Catherine Eddowes	30 September 1888	No anniversary recorded
Mary Kelly	9 November 1888	Prince of Wales's birthday
Annie Farmer	21 November 1888	Empress Frederick's birthday
Rose Mylett	28 December 1888	Feast of the Holy Innocents
Alice MacKenzie	16 July	Fourth Anniversary of the striking of the medal to commemorate the day when Clarence received the Freedom of the City of London
Frances Coles	13 February 1891	The ides of February

A major flaw in the theory is that no anniversaries are attributed to the days two of the Ripper's victims died.

James Stephen was certified as insane in 1891 and died at St Andrew's Hospital, Northampton on 3 February 1892.

Some claim that Stephen's poetry revealed his hatred of women and this can be viewed as an admission concerning the Ripper murders. Judge for yourself:

A Thought

If all the harm that women have done,
were put in a bundle and rolled into one,
Earth would not hold it,
The sky could not enfold it,
It could not be lighted nor warmed by the sun.
Such masses of evil,
Would puzzle the devil,
and keep him in fuel while time's wheels run!

This is an imaginative tale interwoven with the minimum quantity of facts and much reference to blood sacrifice and the Royal calendar. The theory centres around the identity of the mysterious 'S' quoted by Doctor Thomas Stowell. The theory poses more questions than it answers. Why were East End prostitutes selected when the murder of prostitutes in the affluent West End would have caused more embarrassment to the Royal Family? How could Stephen have committed the murders when he had no knowledge of the geography of Whitechapel/Spitalfields?

Sir William Withey Gull

Born: 1816
Occupation: Personal Physician to HRH Queen Victoria.
Died: 29 January 1890.

Continuing the royal theme we reach one of the most popular latter-day Ripper suspects highlighted in a recent television series. Two separate theories involve Gull, neither is particularly probable, but both are worth mentioning.

The first theory and perhaps the most popular, involved Gull and one accomplice. The police who were, of course, at a loss as to who was committing the murders and why, were approached by the famous Spiritualist Robert Lees who had worked in the past for Queen Victoria. Lees described the supposed killer to the police and his mode of transport to and from the murder sites. Lees claimed to have had visions of a Royal coach carrying the Ripper. He later claimed that the coach had tried to run him over. The authorities did not believe Lees, but he later returned and provided information which had been suppressed by the police because if it was released the whole investigation would be jeopardized. Enquiries were made at Buckingham Palace regarding the use of official coaches and the police were told that no coaches were out on the dates concerned. Immediately, the investigating police-officers realized that either Lees was mistaken, or there had been a cover-up.

Senior detectives visited Sir William Gull at his Mayfair home hoping that he would be able to give them an insight into the personality of the man they were looking for. Gull was more than helpful. On leaving his home, the detectives noted a dust-covered black coach pull up outside his home. The outline of the Royal insignia was silhouetted upon the door by dust, and it was clear that at one time it had been affixed to the coach.

The police questioned the driver of the coach who was John Netley, a private coachman employed by Gull. Netley was arrested and forced to chalk the word 'Jews' upon a prison cell wall. He spelt the word 'Juwes'. The police then realized that Netley was not the killer but knew who the killer was. They hatched a plot with Netley to catch the killer in the act of murder.

On a cold damp night, a prostitute walked through the deserted cobbled streets. All at once, the sound of a coach was heard in the distance, it eventually turned into the tiny street and stopped just a few yards from the prostitute. Netley, the driver, alighted from the driving-seat and approached the whore. As soon as he was out of sight of the coach, he exchanged position with Inspector Abberline who was dressed in the same way as the driver. Abberline took the prostitute to the coach whose passenger doors were now open. Without warning a gloved hand appeared and tried to throttle the whore, clutched in another hand was a shiny-bladed knife. Abberline fought the attacker and pulled him from the coach. The attacker was eventually identified as Sir William Gull. Gull was injured in the fight and taken to hospital where his son-in-law, Doctor Theodore Ackland, certified him as insane. The powers that be instructed Abberline that the Ripper's identity must remain a secret and all paperwork relating to the killer's identity was destroyed.

The motive for the murder was that Gull's brain had given way after years of research into acts of murder and how the human mind reacts to it. He had killed an East End prostitute to see what it felt like to murder someone, enjoying the feeling of power he had continued until it drove him mad.

A variant to this theory is that the police asked Robert Lees to track down the killer from the scene of carnage at Millers Court. His extra sense of evil led the police directly to Gull's home. Another variant is that Lees was travelling on an omnibus when a man stepped onto it. Lees sensed evil and knew the man to be the Ripper. As the man alighted from the bus, he was followed by Lees who recognized him as none other than Sir William Gull ...

A truly ingenious and imaginative tale, but one sadly lacking in real fact and evidence. It takes very little effort to disprove the story. It is inconceivable that a coach bearing the Royal insignia could drive around the East End without being seen. Nor is it feasible that a man of Gull's social standing would have conspired with someone as simple as John Netley. The Lees theory with its Spiritualist connection is part of the myth which has been created over the last one hundred years.

The second theory, although incorrect, is factually sound as far as the Ripper side of things go, but elsewhere we are back in fantasyland. It is superbly put together, but major discrepancies soon come to light.

At the time of the Cleveland Street scandal, the Duke of Clarence met an illiterate shop girl by the name of Annie Elizabeth Crooks. Their relationship blossomed, resulting in the birth of an illegitimate child, a girl, in April 1885. The affair was kept secret. Clarence married Crooks at St Saviour's Roman Catholic Church in London and the couple took rooms at 6 Cleveland Street. Some time later, Queen Victoria learnt of the relationship and submitted a secret memorandum to the Home Secretary and the Prime Minister saying that the relationship must be terminated as quickly as possible. The Prime Minister soon entrusted matters to Sir William Gull who hired John Netley and a third party, who was later named as none other than Sir Robert Anderson, head of the Metropolitan Police CID. Sir Robert ensured that the trio remained one step ahead of inquiring police-officers.

Clarence and Annie were kidnapped from 6 Cleveland Street. Clarence was returned to life at court and Annie was taken to Guy's Hospital where Gull carried out an operation to make her simple and forget her liaison with royalty. A life of mental institutes followed until her sad death in 1920.

The illegitimate child was taken to a place of safety by its nannie one Mary Jane Kelly. After a short period of time, Kelly revealed the story to four other Whitechapel prostitutes and together they planned blackmail. One by one the murderous trio hunted down each of the five prostitutes until all who knew of the liaison between a commoner and royalty were dead. With this task complete, the secret is safe for a time. The illegitimate child grew up and married one Joseph Sickert to whom she told her story. He revealed it to an unsuspecting world, but later denied it, explaining that it was a lie.

Even without Sickert's testimony, admitting it all to be a hoax, it is possible to disprove the theory. Sir William Gull died of natural causes in January 1890. Much has been made of the fact that his death certificate was signed by his son-in-law Doctor Ackland, but even though this is against medical ethics, it does not prove that Gull was involved with the Ripper murders. John Netley met a more untimely death in 1903 when his coach struck a stone in Regent's Park. Netley was thrown from the driver's seat and into the path of the galloping horses, one of which kicked him in the head and killed him instantly. The wheels of the coach then ran over his neck and decapitated him.

One must remember that Sir William Gull was seventy-two years old at the time of the Ripper murders. He had already had the misfortune to suffer one heart attack and was something of a slight invalid. Despite his build, he would not have been fit enough physically to commit the murders, and a man with his heart problem would be unlikely to risk further coronary problems. The body of Annie Chapman was found in the rear yard of 29 Hanbury Street. If Gull had killed her in the coach driven by Netley her body would have had to be carried into the rear yard from the street. Annie Chapman was not light and it would have taken two men to carry her dead weight. And finally, when one considers that Chapman was murdered in broad daylight, it is most unlikely that Gull would have taken the risk of being seen.

The next question concerns the mutilations. Even if the conspiracy had to eliminate all the women who were aware of the Royal connection, there was no reason why the murderer should mutilate the bodies. It would have been better for them to disappear discreetly with as little fuss as possible. The Ripper murders were committed by a man with a designed purpose, not by someone who simply wished to silence someone.

Finally, the supposed killer was described as a young man, late twenties to early thirties, moustached and quite smart and inoffensive in his appearance. Gull was a portly man with a receding hairline who could not be confused with a younger man. Netley was a small squat man devoid of facial hair, and in no way could he be classed as smart in appearance. Sir Robert Anderson actually sported a beard! Once again, we are left with nothing but possibilities and assumptions, and definitely no facts.

It is pleasing for me to report that this is the last link with royalty and the Ripper. The Royal Ripper is just a myth, created to appease a world which likes to dream and believe the wholly impossible.

Dr Roslyn D'Onston Stephenson

Born: 1841.
Occupation: Doctor of medicine.
Died: 1912.

A drug-addicted alcoholic, possibly a fraudulent doctor, and a man with an obsession for black magic and satanic rites is as good a description of our next suspect as we will get. Roslyn D'Onston Stephenson was a mythomaniac with a huge ego problem who took great pleasure in telling untruths about himself and his lifestyle. He displayed all the classic traits of someone with an inferiority complex.

Raised in a typical middle-class northern society, Stephenson grew up in Hull on Humberside. As a youngster he worked hard to improve himself. During this period he claimed the title of doctor, though there is little to support his claim. In the early 1880s he left the north of England for London, and by 1888 he was residing in Whitechapel. By this stage of his life he had become heavily influenced by individuals of ill repute. He had also been introduced to and initiated into black magic and devil worship involving the taking of drugs and a heavy consumption of alcohol.

Through black magic, Stephenson met and became acquainted with people of different social standing. Baroness Vittoria Cremers seems to have fallen under his spell and the two became very close friends. It was alleged that Cremers had lesbian tendencies and though something attracted her to the sad doctor from Hull there is no evidence of a sexual relationship.

One of Stephenson's claims to Cremers was that he not only knew the true identity of Jack the Ripper, but knew the killer personally. He would speak at length about the crimes, entering into long-winded discussions about ways of drugging the victims through certain medications. Stephenson claimed that this explained why the victims never screamed when attacked. He also believed that the killer removed certain body organs for a specific purpose, he would take them away from the scene by placing them between his tie and shirt. Speculating further, Stephenson said each murder site was preselected to form the shape of a profane cross, this would eventually allow the killer to make himself invisible through the use of black magic.

Stephenson wrote letters to the press of the day regularly. They would print them enthusiastically, using one of Stephenson's assorted pseudonyms – Doctor Death, Sudden death and his most popular one, Tautriadelta, which translated means 'Cross three triangles'. The actions of this man soon attracted the attention of the police who interviewed him on a number of occasions, though not in direct connection to the crimes but because of his ridiculous claims. He once made a statement to the police informing them that he believed the Ripper was a doctor by the name of Morgan Davies. Davies had been present in a London hospital when Stephenson noticed him re-enacting a typical Ripper murder. Davies had apparently displayed much enthusiasm during the act and, in Stephenson's opinion, tended to know far too much about the crimes. Whether the police actually believed the drug-crazed doctor's claims or not is not known, but since there is no mention of a Morgan Davies in the official police files, it is possible that it was another of Stephenson's fraudulent claims.

In 1912, Vittoria Cremers became business manager to Aleister Crowley who was a recognized black magician. Crowley was informed by Cremers of Stephenson's stories and he released them to the press as an advertisement to the power and importance of black magic. Since released, the stories have been related in a variety of forms and guises, including one which revolves around a box of ties allegedly owned by Stephenson. The box belonged to Vittoria Cremers and it was claimed that some of the ties had visible bloodstains upon them.

Is it possible that this seemingly mad doctor could have been Jack the Ripper? Stephenson certainly liked to impress upon people that he was or could have been the killer, indeed newspaper editor W.T. Stead believed him to be the very man. I find it difficult to believe that the drug-crazed alcoholic doctor was capable of committing the crimes.

In 1904 Stephenson wrote a book, a religious work titled *The*

Patristic Gospels, which in his own words he 'Completed with the aid of the Holy Spirit'. From devout satanist, Stephenson crossed the threshold into devout Christianity, changing his allegiance from the Devil to Christ. Once again, Stephenson's profound statements display a need to impress.

The claim that the murder sites were preselected to form the shape of a profane cross is nonsensical. This may be the case if one positions the sites incorrectly, but when they are accurately placed upon a map of Whitechapel they form no recognizable shape whatsoever. This is no more than another sensational claim made to shock a naïve Victorian society. Thankfully, we are wise to such personalities in this day and age and can see Stephenson for what he was.

Stephenson was hardly in peak physical condition, his body had been subjected to many years' abuse through drugs and alcohol, his reaction time would have deteriorated thus slowing his responses. He would be hardly have been able to make speedy and deliberate escapes from the scenes of the murders or had the strength to carry out the mutilations. Stephenson has none of the attributes associated with Jack the Ripper, there is not the slightest indication of physical violence in his actions. Doctor Roslyn D'Onston Stephenson was a man whose world had been turned upside down and inside out through his perpetual lies, eventually he found it difficult to differentiate between fact and fiction, ultimately he became a vagrant within his own land of mythology. His claims to be Jack the Ripper are just one part of this unfortunate man's egotistical desire for power and fame. Stephenson was psychologically a small man who strived for notoriety.

Dr Alexander Pedachenko, alias Vassily Konovalov and possibly Michael Ostrog

Born: 1857.
Occupation: Doctor.
Died: 1908.

This theory was revealed in 1923 by William LeQueux, who claimed to have read manuscripts penned by the mad monk, Rasputin. The papers were said to have been recorded in French

and hidden in the cellar of Rasputin's home.

The story which it was claimed Rasputin had recorded is as follows. A lunatic Russian doctor was an accomplished murderer who had seen off a number of women in his home town of Tver, was employed by the Russian secret service who sent him to London so that he could commit similar atrocities thus embarrassing the British authorities. Hence the Whitechapel murders were carried out.

This claim was assessed by author Donald McCormick who published his conclusions in his 1959 book *The Identity of Jack the Ripper*. McCormick claims that Doctor Thomas Dutton recorded in the mysterious *Chronicles of Crime* information which was relevant to the Ripper inquiry, concerning an individual named Pedachenko. Dutton, it seems, was convinced that this man was Jack the Ripper and revealed the basis for this conviction in the *Chronicles*. Since the *Chronicles* are now missing, it is now impossible to confirm or deny this though McCormick claims to have seen the Dutton work and explains it.

Johann Nideroest was an active member of the Jubilee Club, more commonly known as the Anarchist Centre of the East End. Nideroest claimed Pedachenko was the Ripper and stated that he lived in Westmoreland Street, Walworth. From there, he would travel to his nights of pleasure in Whitechapel by omnibus and then on foot. He was assisted by two accomplices, a man called Levitski and a woman called Winberg. Winberg would engage the selected victims in conversation while Pedachenko would creep up behind the unsuspecting woman and slit her throat, while all this was taking place Levitski would keep watch.

Once sufficient murders had been committed, Pedachenko and his two accomplices were smuggled out of the country and back to Russia, where Levitski and Winberg were exiled to Yakutsk. It further appears that Doctor Dutton stated that Inspector Abberline believed Pedachenko and George Chapman were the same person. McCormick then reveals his ultimate evidence by describing a translation of the *Ochrana*, the secret newspaper of the Russian secret service, dated January 1909. This reported that Pedachenko, alias Vassily Konovalov and Andrey Luiskovo, was officially dead, and that he was the man wanted for the murder of five women in the east quarter of London in 1888 and for murder in Petrograd in 1891.

Here at last is some firm evidence leading to a particular individual – surely there can be no doubt about the authenticity of this document? However, serious discrepancies contained within the document are difficult, if not impossible, to explain away. The translation of the *Ochrana* which McCormick claims to have seen was dated January 1909 and refers to murder in Petrograd. Petrograd was not so named until 1914, it was then St Petersburg.

Further problems arise when one refers to Richard Deacon's *History of the Russian Secret Service* (London, 1972). Deacon quotes the *Ochrana* in a section on the crimes of Jack the Ripper, and states that it revealed Pedachenko was also known as Konovalov, Luiskovo and Michael Ostrog. The latter is a revelation, for McCormick makes no mention to this name in his book published in 1959 and he would surely not have omitted a name? Further research reveals a possible answer to this. The name Michael Ostrog first appeared late in 1959 in the notes of Sir Melville MacNaghton. McCormick's book was actually published before MacNaghton's comments were released to the public. Richard Deacon makes no attempt to hide the fact that he is in fact Donald McCormick. McCormick failed to add Ostrog to his 1959 work because he did not know he existed. Any confusion is not solely the responsibility of Donald McCormick (whose work is of excellent value to all would-be Ripper researchers) but of its originator, William LeQueux. This individual appears to have told untruths deliberately, for example, he claimed that the Rasputin manuscript which he located in the cellar of the mad monk's home had been penned by Rasputin in French. Yet there is evidence which states that Rasputin could not speak French and he lived in a first-floor flat which had no cellar. We are forced to the conclusion that the Russian secret service theory is no more than a fictional account of the facts after the murders. It fails to stand up to any sort of scrutiny and is of little value.

Kosminski

Details unknown due to the large number of Kosminskis in the area during the period.

Kosminski's name is officially mentioned in the MacNaghton papers in the official police file, yet the theory surrounding him is shrouded in a veil of mystery. In the MacNaghton papers Kosminski is given no Christian name, which creates vast problems for the researcher; however, theories about him abound – all from just a few lines in the police file:

> Kosminski, a Polish Jew, residing in Whitechapel. This man became insane owing to many years of indulgence in solitary vices. He had a great hatred of women, especially the prostitute class, and had strong homicidal tendencies; he was removed to a lunatic asylum about March 1889. There were many circs connected which made him a strong suspect.

Sir Robert Anderson, then head of CID, stated;

> During my absence abroad the Police had made house to house searches for him, investigating the case of every man in the district whose circumstances were such that he could go and come and get rid of bloodstains in secret. And the conclusion we came to was that he and his people were certain low class Polish Jews; for it is remarkable that people of that class in the East End will not give up one of their number to Gentile justice. And the result proved that our diagnosis was right on every point ... I will merely add that the only person who ever had a good view of the murderer unhesitatingly identified the suspect the instant he was confronted with him, but he refused to give evidence against him. In saying that he was a Polish Jew I am merely stating a definitely ascertained fact. And my words are meant to specify race, not religion.

Direct information supplied by a senior police official of the time has to be deemed accurate, however, I object to Anderson's suggestion that the police and other authorities were fully aware of the killer's identity yet could prove no case against him and thereby allowed him to walk the streets a free man. This does not marry with the fact that the official police files remained open until 1892, nor does it explain why a witness who identified the individual was permitted to refrain from giving evidence against him. The comments made by Anderson are trivial, an attempt to promote a false belief that he knew the identity of the man wanted.

In the late 1980s, Scotland Yard received some personal

papers belonging to Chief Inspector Donald Swanson, among these papers was a copy of Anderson's book with scribbled comments in the margins of a number of pages. The marginalia are allegedly in the hand of Swanson, but their purpose remains as mysterious as the killings themselves. The comments concern Kosminski and name him as being the number one suspect and state that due to insufficient police evidence no action was taken against him. The notes also record that Kosminski passed away at Colney Hatch lunatic asylum in 1889 or shortly afterwards. This is a little ambiguous for my liking and I feel suspicious about the authenticity of the notes and their accuracy. It is unlikely a detective interested in the case would forget such a memorable date as the one on which Jack the Ripper died. However, these 'official' notes do provide the place of death. Research shows that the only Kosminski to die in a lunatic asylum between 1888 and 1924 was Aaron Kosminski who must, therefore, be the individual named by Swanson and MacNaghton and also referred to by Anderson.

Aaron Kosminski was admitted to Colney Hatch lunatic asylum on 7 January 1891 having previously received treatment at Mile End Old Town workhouse in July 1890. According to official records he practised self-abuse, refused to wash and was told by voices within his head not to accept food from people. Because of this he chose to walk the streets picking food from the gutters and harbouring a deep mistrust of anyone who approached him. The officials at Colney Hatch described Kosminski as being neither dangerous to himself or to anyone else. There is no official reference to him being suspected of the Ripper murders. It would have been professional practice to mention somewhere in his case file that he was suspected of being a homicidal maniac of the most dangerous type and that no female member of staff should be allowed to approach him alone. There is absolutely nothing which would indicate that Kosminski was a Ripper suspect. If he was, it seems odd that the police chose to take no action after the Millers Court carnage which had sickened so many officers and caused renewed commitment to the attempt to bring the killer to justice. It is in the extreme unlikely that the police shown have known who he was and let him wander around the East End for a further two years.

Swanson's marginalia claims that Kosminski died shortly after being admitted to the asylum. Aaron Kosminski was discharged from Colney Hatch on 19 April 1894 and transferred to Leavesden, where he died on 24 March 1919 from gangrene. If Kosminski was such a strong suspect then how is it that police officials know so little about the date and place of his death. One must ask what Swanson hoped to gain by pencilling vital evidence relating to the Ripper murders in the margin of a book rather than police files. The statement that Kosminski was not picked up until 1891 further confuses matters. Swanson claims that his suspect was mentally disturbed, but if this is so it becomes difficult to explain why he ceased his reign of terror. Being mentally abnormal he would have been confused about times and dates and would not have been able to decide when to stop or to hide, Kosminski would have been quite reckless about whether he would be apprehended.

Other variants of the Kosminski theory have been put forward in recent years. Both Nathan Kaminsky and Martin Kosminski have been named as the killer referred to by the police-officers. Neither man is recorded as having died during this period and they can therefore be disregarded as suspects. David Cohen is another name which has been attributed to Kosminski, the explanation being that he was given this name by the authorities since he could not remember his own identity. Factually this assumption is sound as Cohen died in 1889, but there the link ends. If he had been the man then he would surely have been named in the police files.

As with so many other theories there is a high proportion of discrepancies in the Kosminski case. The final comment upon this individual has to come from the police files and Sir Melville MacNaghton who believed that, 'This man became insane owing to many years indulgence in solitary vices.' In common terms, he became insane through masturbating too frequently. Such a statement cannot be taken seriously today. Kosminski is just another name in the file.

Dr Merchant

Born: 1851.
Occupation: Doctor.
Died: December 1888.

A totally new suspect came to light in 1931, when the *Daily Express* published a letter from a retired Metropolitan police constable by the name of Robert Spicer, who claimed to have served in Whitechapel during the Ripper investigations. The letter was titled 'I Caught Jack the Ripper'. It told how Spicer was on foot patrol in Brick Lane on the night of 30 September 1888 when, on turning into Henage Street, he came to a small court some fifty yards along the street called Henage Court. Constable Spicer walked into the gloomy little alley and saw a prostitute whom he had come to know through his patrols sitting upon a brick dustbin. Standing beside her was a rather tall distinguished-looking gentleman holding a Gladstone bag. The sharp-eyed constable spotted bloodstains on the cuffs of the man's shirt and immediately asked him how he came by these stains. The man advised him that it was none of his business. The constable then arrested the man and without further delay took him back to Commercial Street police station, with the prostitute following close behind. Spicer took the man before the duty inspector and explained the circumstances surrounding the arrest. The senior officer approached the man and requested some form of identification, he showed the inspector a card and, after polite questioning, was allowed to leave the station and return from whence he came. No check or search of the Gladstone bag was made and one feels that the constable felt hard done by since his hunch had failed; to make matters worse, the duty inspector verbally reprimanded Spicer for arresting someone on such flimsy evidence. Spicer claimed he had become disillusioned by this affair, but continued his vigilance in the streets.

Over a period of time he claimed to have seen the man in the vicinity of Liverpool Street railway station on a number of occasions. Usually, he was in the act of accosting women, indeed on one occasion Spicer claimed to have approached the man and say, 'Hello Jack, still after them?' Not surprisingly, he claimed that the victim of his scathing comments fled the area. Shortly after this incident, Spicer resigned from the Metropolitan Police.

Research into Spicer's claims was carried out by journalist Brian E. Reilly and he concluded that the man was a Doctor Merchant who died of tuberculosis in December 1888. Reilly believed that Merchant knew he was terminally ill, he embarked on a campaign of revenge upon unfortunate prostitutes whom he blamed as the cause of his illness. Quite correctly, Reilly claimed that the Ripper's actions were those of a desperate man, and he felt that Doctor Merchant was a desperate man, terminally ill and reckless as to risks and dangers. The research carried out by Reilly is superbly accurate and most impressive, he names a good suspect with a fair motive. The flaw is that it relies one hundred per cent upon the testimony of Robert Spicer, and if this is incorrect then Reilly's theory is exposed as false.

My first concern regards the duty inspector who allowed Spicer's suspect to walk from the police station on the night of the 'double event' without carrying out a proper investigation, this was and indeed still remains a serious breach of the Police Discipline regulations. The only excuse for his actions has to be that the said suspect had already been the subject of police enquiries, and that the inspector was fully aware of this fact and elected to release the man since continuing with pointless investigations would mean one less patrolling officer on the streets. Spicer, of course, had only been drafted into the district a few weeks earlier and would not have been fully conversant with everyone who had been arrested and questioned.

From a professional point of view, Spicer's actions and attitude leave a great deal to be desired. He openly confesses to taunting an unknown member of the public and accusing him of being the Ripper. This is an abuse of authority and if Spicer's supervisors had been aware of his actions they would have been forced to resign as an alternative to being sacked. Further insight into Spicer's attitude arises from his comment in the letter published in the *Daily Express*, that he had seen his suspect accosting women (one of the alleged traits of the Ripper) yet chose not to arrest him. It is as well that not all the police-officers of 1888 were as lackadaisical as Spicer as no crime would have been detected. Is it any wonder that the Ripper was able to escape detection when officers displaying the attitude of Robert Spicer patrolled the streets. Spicer broke almost every rule in the book, failing to report or to take action on the nefarious activities of another person. It certainly seems that he had become opposed to the authoritarian attitude displayed in the police service, and perhaps these recollections, printed some forty years after the event, were a form of revenge for those occasions when his information was seemingly ignored by serving police-officers.

It may well be that the story depicted by Spicer was accurate and has an element of truth behind it, but final consideration must be given to the prostitute who sat with Spicer's suspect in Henage Court. It should be remembered that she followed Spicer to the police station, but made no complaint or displayed any suspicion of the man. It would appear that she went to the station in order to clear him for a police station was not one of the most popular venues for a prostitute to attend voluntarily.

I do admire Reilly's research and work in producing this theory, but it is based upon the opinions of an ex-policeman who was not, it seems, particularly good at his job. What credibility can be given to Spicer's claims? The answer is ... none.

Dr Stanley

Pure Fictional Character.

The Doctor Stanley theory was invented in 1929 when it was released as the first complete theory published upon the crimes of Jack the Ripper. The book was aptly titled *The Mystery of Jack the Ripper*, and was divided into two separate parts, fact and fiction (or theory). The factual aspect is well presented but lacks much in the way of real evidence and detail and there are those typical discrepancies which tend to confuse and mystify the reader, but considering the limited data then available it is a credit to its author Leonard Matters. This book laid the foundations for all the Ripper books which were to follow as the lay-out of each new title is similar to that of Matters' work.

The theoretical (fictional) side of the work is hardly credible, but is highly controversial in its subversive inferences about the medical profession. Doctor Stanley, states the theory, a top Harley Street surgeon with a reputation second to none whose son contracted venereal disease in the form of syphilis. This was caught from a Whitechapel prostitute by the name of Mary Jane Kelly. The son eventually died from the effects of the disease and Doctor Stanley swore his revenge upon the Kelly woman and set out to track her down.

The immediate problem Stanley encountered was that Mary Kelly used so many aliases. He has great difficulty in ascertaining which prostitute is Kelly, and the first four murders can be written off as cases of mistaken identity. Eventually though, Stanley finds his prey and carried out the Millers Court atrocity. On completion of the crusade, Stanley emigrated to Buenos Aires in South America where he resumed his medical work. Many years later, he revealed his morbid secret to a young student who released it to the world.

Study of the medical registers and other documents quickly reveals that no such person as Doctor Stanley existed at this time. This completely destroys Matters' theory, as do a number of other factors. It is claimed that Doctor Stanley's son died of syphilis yet, although no known cure existed at the time, there were certain medications available which could retard the disease and extend the life of the sufferer. It is unbelievable that Stanley, a top-class Harley Street surgeon with professional knowledge and contacts, would not use all of his resources to fight the disease. Furthermore, it is claimed that the son contracted the disease from Mary Kelly, yet inquest reports make no mention that Kelly suffered from venereal disease.

To be fair to Matters, he states at the beginning of his book, 'How can this mystery ever be solved, when nobody seemed to be careful about the facts before attempting to suggest a solution?' The author knew that he was not providing a solution, but merely pointing an accusing finger at a certain class of individual who may have been capable of committing such acts.

Persons Unidentified

Butcher/Slaughterman

The belief that the Ripper might have belonged to this profession was extremely rife during the times of the murders, when various officials claimed that the injuries sustained were similar to those a butcher or slaughterman would inflict upon a dead animal. Various police enquiries were made at all such establishments resulting in a variety of arrests.

On 12 September 1888, just four days after the murder of

Annie Chapman, Joseph Isenschmid, a pork butcher, was arrested and would possibly have been condemned had not other Ripper murders been committed while he was being held in prison. Isenschmid was arrested after information received from his local innkeeper at the Prince Albert public house in Brushfield Street. The alert woman told the police that a man wearing a stiff brown coat and hat had been in her pub around seven o'clock on the morning of Annie Chapman's death. The stranger had had blood on his hands and was acting in a suspicious manner. Police inquiries soon led to Isenschmid's wife who volunteered the information that she had not seen her husband for almost two months and, for good measure, added that he normally carried knives around with him. On his arrest, several prostitutes told the police that Isenschmid was a prostitute-hater and he was alleged to have told many people that his nickname was 'Leather Apron'. Subsequent interviews with Butcher Isenschmid revealed that he was mentally subnormal. He was admitted to Bow Infirmary Asylum in Fairfield Road for examination, and questioned on several subsequent occasions by police. Eventually though, they forgot about poor Isenschmid who lived out his life in asylums and madhouses before dying in obscurity, a victim of society and of mistaken identity.

Police enquiries turned to the abundant number of slaughterhouses and other such establishments in the district, some streets had as many as five within their boundaries. The role of the slaughterman would provide a perfect disguise for a would-be Ripper for dozens of blood-covered slaughtermen openly walked the streets during the normal course of the day.

With people of so many different religions living in this community, there was a wide variety of slaughterman and slaughtering techniques. The most common was the Jewish shochet who followed the rituals for slaughtering laid down in Talmudic law involving the slaughterer (shochet), his knife (khalef) and the actual act itself (shechita). The selected animal was prepared by ritual and the shochet would then draw the khalef across the sacrifice's throat with one swift back-and-forth movement. This would cause a great gash in the animal's throat and allow the bright red blood to flow freely from the wound. Once the animal was dead, which took very little time, a post-mortem (bedikah) would take place in which the chest and abdomen being slit open allowing a full internal check of the vital organs. If the animal was passed as fit (kosher), it was butchered into manageable parts.

Shochets were classed as a religious order and were normally ordained priests. Their own people saw them as above reprisal and would report them should they transgress the English criminal law. Few shochets would be tempted to commit such acts as they were financially and socially secure. There are certain similarities between the slaughtering of an animal in the shechita method and the Ripper murders. The press of 1888 made much of this connection.

A letter in the *Illustrated Police News* reported in 1884 that a Jew living in a small village near Cracow had committed a sexual act with a Christian woman and then murdered her. The anti-semitic press claimed that in Jewish religion this sexual act was classed as a sin and the only way in which the man could atone for the misdemeanour was to destroy the object of his affection, in this case the Christian woman. There is no evidence to substantiate this claim. The press felt that this was a logical explanation for the murder, but failed to inject any further comment on the subject.

Both butcher and slaughterman theories have much in their favour, but both lack real evidence and fail to supply a motive. The suggestion that either occupation could become bored with cutting-up animals and turned to human kind is absurd, as there is a massive difference between butchering an animal and a human being. The theories surrounding the men of this particular occupation are speculative, none of the hard evidence available even points us in this direction.

Policeman Ripper

The idea of a policeman Jack the Ripper is a theory full of promise and real interest. After all, the entire district was crawling with police-officers from all over the City, many of whom were not the law-abiding citizens they should have been; that is not to say that all policemen were crooked, but there is certainly evidence that a few men were as corrupt as the villains they were employed to catch. The policeman disguise would place the Ripper in an ideal situation, the women of the street would have felt reassured that he was there, and they would hardly be likely to identify a bogus official among the numbers who were present.

Officially an on-duty police-officer would not or could not partake in any sexual activity or contact with any person, that is not to say that it did not occur, but it was officially forbidden. In order to identify the Policeman Ripper, we must define a certain individual type who would risk a bogus sexual encounter in order to get the victim where he wanted her. It may well be that patrolling police-officers commonly engaged in conversation with prostitutes. This would also assist the Ripper in his attack as the woman's defence would have been lowered in the confident presence of a policeman. It is certain that a policeman's disguise would have been of great assistance to the Ripper after the Mitre Square murder when dozens of uniformed officers were descending upon the tiny square. An officer in a uniform could easily pass through the advancing ranks without causing too much comment.

It is there that this theory falls apart. No uniformed officer would dare walk along Dorset Street alone, and would certainly have thought twice about entering a prostitute's room alone. The Policeman Ripper would have had the ideal disguise but very little else. The weather conditions of that autumn were particularly severe, with a number of people dying in the streets of hypothermia. The autumn nights were bitterly cold and patrolling police-officers would be forced to wear the regulation heavy greatcoat, a garment of thick wool interwoven with synthetic fibre similar to a woollen blanket. The coat thoroughly restricts movement and it would be impossible to move with any speed or dexterity. I can confirm that since I wore such a coat for many years.

It would be almost impossible to take anyone by surprise whilst wearing such a coat, and this greatly reduces the likelihood that the Ripper could have been a policeman. The cynics may well say that a policeman could have taken his coat off or not worn his greatcoat. This again is speculation, the weather was cold and no policeman would patrol in his tunic, it was easier to wear the coat than to carry it. Furthermore, the Victorian policeman wore a thick leather belt around the waist of the coat, the Ripper would have been most unlikely to go through the hassle of fastening and unfastening the buckle, for him time was of the essence.

The Policeman Ripper theory may be fine for fictional accounts, but in reality was an impossibility. It was initially proposed by the press in a political statement to increase the pressure upon the authorities. It has never been seriously accepted, had it been so, then all kinds of social problems would have arisen. A murdering policeman would cause serious problems in the roots of our society.

The Lodger

This theory has been repeated in dozens of different forms. Stage plays, and even feature films, have been based upon it. It is perhaps the archetypal image of Jack the Ripper, with a varying storyline depending on what effect the respective producer wished to propose.

In order to understand this theory, we must describe the background information and set the scene. Imagine then, damp cobbled streets, flickering gas-lamps and a thick dense fog which refuses to lift. Among all this we can hear the incessant sound of horses' hooves as they echo around the deserted streets. The next scene depicts an ordinary guest-house in an ordinary street which is owned by a pair of normal elderly people. Late one evening there comes a knock at the door. The landlord opens it and a gush of freezing cold fog rushes into the room, as this clears away the old man sees a stranger on his doorstep, a man wearing a top hat, cloak and – you guessed it – carrying a Gladstone bag! The man asks for a room and the landlord is able to provide him with one. The stranger pays three weeks' rent in advance and goes to his room. At first the couple think of him as a nice young man who causes them little or no problems; but suddenly he begins to act strangely and keeps odd hours, returning home at three or four o'clock in the morning. Eventually the old man asks him why he keeps such late hours and the stranger explains that it is due to his occupation as a medical student at a nearby hospital. Over the weeks which follow the man becomes obsessed with the Whitechapel murders, which are headline news in all the daily newspapers, he reads the reports with great enthusiasm and fervour.

One day the stranger goes out and the old man enters his room. There he finds much bloodstained clothing and a set of knives! The police are informed, but before they arrive, the stranger returns and senses something is wrong. He immediately packs his bags and leaves, disappearing into the thick fog. Sometime later the landlord sees the man walking in a nearby street, he speaks to him, but the stranger ignores him. The landlord runs to inform a patrolling policeman, the officer chases the stranger who runs away from his pursuer. Eventually the chase ends upon London Bridge where the killer falls or jumps into the icy depths of the fog-bound river and to his certain death.

Although this sounds farcical, a similar sequence of events actually took place during the Ripper enquiry. The accused was a Mr G. Wentworth Bell Smith from Toronto, Canada. In August 1888 he was accused of keeping loaded revolvers in his rooms at 27 Sun Street, Finsbury Square. It is not known if he had a firearms certificate and his landlord may have felt loaded firearms were a threat, but since he was later released it seems his possession was legitimate. The police investigated the matter and found him to be a religious zealot with a deep hatred for prostitutes and women of the street. They did not, however, consider he was dangerous, nor did they suspect him of any other criminal offences. News of this incident came to Doctor Forbes Winslow, an amateur detective, who decided to investigate the matter further. He claimed that he had received information that the Mr Wentworth Bell Smith did not return to his rooms until 4.00 a.m. on the morning of Martha Tabram's (Turner) murder. The same afternoon, the landlord of his lodgings had entered his room and found a pair of cut-down rubber boots which were covered in blood. Winslow took possession of these and informed the press of his find. The police were asked to examine the boots, this they did, but found no traces of blood though they did say there was a good deal of mud, so it could once again have been misinterpreted. Winslow was furious that the police should mock his detective work, and attempted to exact his revenge through the press whom he told that he had arranged to meet the Ripper on the steps of St Paul's Cathedral. In order to make this more dramatic he also added that he had informed the police of these facts, but they had ignored everything he said. This suggested that the police were not interested in apprehending the Ripper. The press revelled in such statements and duly printed Winslow's feelings; the police were horrified by the comments and paid Winslow a personal visit to find out why he was telling untruths to the press. Winslow denied saying anything to the press and fully blamed bad journalism for the allegations of police stupidity. Winslow made no further dramatic statements to the press and his interest in the Ripper murders diminished after the police visit. Needless to say, Mr Wentworth Bell Smith was in no way connected with the Ripper and was free from further allegations.

There is a thin dividing line between fact and fiction in many of the theories we have just examined. That not one was able to stand up to close scrutiny is no fault of their respective authors, but in the fact that not many authors have experience of or access to the day-to-day running of a police enquiry and lack professional knowledge of police matters. Theories become complicated and difficult to believe. Only the author knows how accurate his research has been and whether he has the evidence to feel confident that he is correct. I appreciate that much of what has been written on the Ripper is mythical, and that a certain amount of the legend must remain intact as it has been passed down from generation to generation, but it is not difficult to find the truth as I first feared, though it is possible to get drawn into the mire and lost in the legend.

The Whitechapel murders were committed for a specific purpose, like all murders they had a motive. Jack the Ripper was a real everyday person who lived and breathed the same air as many of his victims, he lived among and walked upon the same streets as his prey, yet nothing around him aroused suspicion; but there were those who had their doubts about his personality and attitude, especially those close to him, of which there were few. Jack the Ripper cried out for attention, he needed to be loved and wanted, he required a woman to love him in much the same way his mother had, indeed his ideal woman would have been in the image of his dead mother. As the saying goes, 'People do the strangest things', especially for love.

5 So who was Jack the Ripper?

Having discussed in some detail the theories concerning those who have been suspected of being the Ripper it is evident that none of the aforementioned suspects are remotely connected with the Whitechapel murders of 1888. In this chapter I intend to explain the mystery which has baffled the world for over 102 years, and will first consider the psychological features which will identify our man. I have been extremely fortunate in receiving vital documents concerning the psychology of the criminal mind from the American Federal Bureau of Investigation (FBI) who have analysed serial murderers whose crimes have a similar orientation to the Victorian Ripper's. The results of this research are amazing and will go a long way in assisting investigating authorities in identifying particular traits with particular criminal classes. The research is based on interviews with about fifty mass murderers which attempt to build pictures of their lives from childhood to the day of the murders right up to arrest. From this data the profilers were able to identify certain events in the criminals' make-up which were influential to their criminal orientation.

The murders of Jack the Ripper have been proclaimed as the first sexually oriented murders committed in criminal history. I disagree with this conclusion as in August 1807 a common prostitute known as Ann Webb (Elizabeth Winterflood) was found murdered among some coster barrows in Higglers Lane, London. The positioning of the body and the injuries sustained during the attack were similar to the latter-day Ripper crimes. A police report on the case contains the following passage, describing the wounds inflicted:

> Legs wide apart, left one bent at the knee. Long dress pulled above waistline, displaying lower sexual regions which had been

> subjected to mutilation with some form of sharp blade. Various pieces of body tissue being absent, internal organs visible.

Shortly after the body had been found and examined by the police surgeons, flesh from the vagina was found beneath a nearby coster barrow. This crime took place some eighty-one years before those of Jack the Ripper, and it is obviously sexually orientated. The positioning of the body displays the classic 'supreme master' syndrome in which the killer displays his power over the victim by leaving the body in a humiliating pose, with the savage butchery clear to all who view the body. The killer of Ann Webb was never brought to justice, but it was generally believed that she had suffered at the hands of her ex-lover with whom she had quarrelled some days prior to her death.

In the pioneering days of police investigations and medical assessment much in the way of research was carried out concerning individual identification traits which were assumed to be present in all criminal types. Plaster casts of the heads of serious felons who were hanged were made after execution. Those 'death masks' were made so that the various lumps or bumps which were present on the head, could be compared with similar marks on the head of another criminal of a similar type. Naturally the system failed, but it provides an insight into the fact that Victorian investigators realized that there had to be a reason why these individuals committed crimes.

With present-day technology it is possible to simplify the characteristics of an individual murderer, but we must not lose track of the basis of the human mind. Murder is present within all of us as witness the frequent exclamation, 'I will kill him/her'. This is an emotional state caused by circumstances, but each of us has the free-will to control such emotions. It is when we choose to relax or lose control, that problems arise and emotions take over and control our actions. People who cannot control such emotions are easily recognizable since criminal tendencies usually display themselves at an early age, hopefully corrective remedies will resolve the problem. Yet others cannot control spasmodic emotional reactions, and though for the majority of the time they are rational, they are the murderers among us.

Murder is committed for a designated purpose or reason. These can be subdivided into five separate categories which cover almost every aspect of possible motive:

Gain: This can be for financial gain or other materialistic goods which the killer would thereby obtain. The killer generally premeditates the attack to ensure that the required benefits are established.

Revenge: A premeditated attack to compensate for some form of personal grievance.

Jealousy: A form of retribution committed by a person who often feels insecure about a situation or relationship. In many cases the killer tends to be a loner, or separate from what is taking place in the normal day-to-day routine around him.

Elimination: To eliminate another person's existence.

Lust: The worst type of killer, with no motive or purpose other than a psychological problem which causes them to kill at random. This type of killer usually enjoys the emotional experience and satisfaction gained during the commission of the crime, and this makes them kill again and again.

Analysing this data in relation to the crimes of the Ripper, we arrive at just one motive which can be linked to the crimes, that of *Jealousy*. None of the other motives are identifiable. *Lust* killings would have continued for a longer period and would have been committed with much more greater frequency. *Elimination* is not feasible, since no one would hope to gain anything by murdering an East End whore. Similarly, *Gain* has no obvious advantages in the district where the crimes took place. All that is left is *Jealousy*, and such crimes can take place in all kinds of social circles.

With the knowledge of why murder is committed established, the second factor is the question is who commits murder. The initial answer to this may surprise a few people, but it is a fact that anyone can kill depending upon the circumstances. However, we can once again categorize and subdivide killer types into three main categories relating to the set psychological aspects:

Schizophrenic: Individuals who have at one time suffered some kind of psychotic disorder and are categorized by progressive deterioration of the personality. They generally suffer from hallucinations and feelings of emotional instability. A rare breed of killer.

Monomaniac: People who possess an excessive mental preoccupation with one person or subject. This turns into an obsession and completely takes over their life causing confusion.

Psychopath: The most common type of killer, particularly mass murderers. They are normally persons who have suffered some form of antisocial disease. Afflicted with personality disorders, they have a tendency to commit violent acts. They feel no remorse for their actions.

It is without doubt that Jack the Ripper belonged to the last category of killer, as the social conditions of the East End were not favourable to the other categories. Suddenly, for the first time in history, we can cross the threshold of guess-work and assumptions, now we can identify a specific character type as that of Jack the Ripper.

With the benefit of the literature provided by the FBI, I have been able to study and analyse the particular social traits of the type of man we are looking for. The guidelines provided by the FBI state that a murderer who kills on more than three occasions is classed as a 'serial killer'. In between these crimes there is an emotional cooling-off period which permits the emotional stress to subside, eventually the killer selects another victim, and so on. The antecedents of such individuals have been defined with alarming accuracy and are as follows.

The murderer usually began life in a two-parent family home of average economic stature. The mother remained within the family environment to look after the family, while the father was regularly employed with a solid working background. Because the father was absent from home for long periods of time due to working commitments, the child generally lacked parental guidance or, at the very least, consistent discipline. The killer often lived with another person before the crime, normally with a woman. The crimes would commence after some form of stressful event occurred in his life. The killer normally remained aloof of his surroundings preferring his own company. The crimes committed would take place near to his home, where there was a feeling of insecurity caused by the instability of his home life in the late 1880s. The victims of such a killer would be grossly mutilated, and the killer seldom using an impersonal weapon (such as a firearm) to commit the crime, he would prefer to use brute force and a pointed weapon. Facial disfigurement of the victim often means that the killer knew the victim, and the killer will often follow the criminal investigation in the press. The victims will all come from a similar social background and are of a similar type. The killer never leaves clues at the scene of the crime.

This is the data as recorded in the volumes of FBI material. It is not an interpretation of the facts which I have made to further the case against my suspect. The traits mentioned are those of killers similar to Jack the Ripper and, as will be seen, fit directly with the individual to be named in this book.

There is evidence which proves that the Ripper crimes cannot have been as complicated or complex as proposed in other theories. Factual data dictates that the majority of murders are committed by individuals who are known to the victim, often a lover or personal friend. Armed with much of this data, we can now commence the search for Jack the Ripper.

When I first began research into this series of murders, I have to confess to being somewhat naïve when it came to selecting a suspect. I had no single individual in mind, nor had I the magic formula at my fingertips which would enable me to produce such a person. Any named suspect was selected from the years of research into police documents relating to the Whitechapel murders and other such cases, as well as the professional knowledge gained through practical policing. Initially I believed that it would be to my advantage that I did not have a named suspect in mind. In reality I have to admit that it made matters more difficult, as it meant I had to research into everyone else's suspects in the vain hope that I might come across some piece of influential evidence that had been previously overlooked. Sadly, all that I was left with was the broken dreams of other researchers. The one purpose served by this was that I narrowed the field of suspects drastically. I was continually reminded that a policeman's logic would pay dividends provided I continued to be thorough in my research techniques; slowly, the suspects were eliminated, and I reasoned that to continue in the same manner using basic questions would eventually provide the solution.

The very subject of the investigation is a rather mundane murder case, as far as murder cases now go. Five common East End prostitutes of the worst possible character were butchered. To believe that a complicated reason lay behind this scenario is ridiculous. As we have seen, murder is always committed for a reason, but locating the reason caused me some grief. My first thoughts concerned the murdered women. It seems foolish to believe that they were not known to each other; after all, they had all lived in the same street, drunk in the same pubs, and even used each other's names from time to time. As well as this, they were all prostitutes, and knowing how close-knit the East End was at that time, it would take a brave man to deny that the women knew each other. After all, what are the odds against a killer disposing of five East End prostitutes out of almost two thousand and selecting five who live, drink and work together. With this established, I was able to commence my search for a suspect and scrutinized every available document which exists on the case, either officially or otherwise. Armed with every name mentioned in police files, books, notes and every other available source, I set about investigating each named person, one by one.

The first person to attract my attention was the carman 'Cross' who, by his own admission, had been seen standing over the body of Polly Nichols, the first victim, in Bucks Row. My suspicions were aroused since he was the only individual to be seen near the body of a victim, initially it appeared that his actions were not those of an innocent man. Cross told the police that as he stood over the body in Bucks Row he heard footsteps approaching from behind, in a panic he stood back in the shadows and hid from the approaching person. I was puzzled why he hid. Surely an innocent person would not act in such a way. Did he hide to escape detection or did he hide from fear? Cross claimed that he hid because he thought the footsteps might have belonged to the woman's attacker who was returning for a second attack.

My second suspicion concerned the reasoning behind his unhealthy interest in the woman. He must have walked past dozens of drunken whores in Whitechapel before, so why was he curious about this one. In truth, the actions of Mr Cross are suspicious and it would be all too easy to build a case against him. The evidence we have here cannot be denied – this alone is more than we have previously ascertained against any other suspect. Although it is easy to create evidence against Cross, there is little information about his antecedents. Frantic research has provided no reason for Cross to kill Polly Nichols, or any further evidence implicating him deeper in the enquiry. His suspicious actions must be explained away by natural human emotions. There is no man on this earth who would act naturally when finding the bloody body of a woman in the street. I realized that Cross was in no way involved, other than as a witness. It does surprise me that he has not before been promoted as a first-rate suspect, as he is a more likely suspect than many others previously named.

With Cross eliminated, I was left with six names upon my list, with many other suspects flitting in and out of the investigation as it progressed, witnesses, friends and petty criminals, even police officials. The majority are nothing more than names added to the files for official witness purposes; others were people who wanted the ill-gotten glory of being mentioned in the press or who were questioned by the police about false information they had supplied.

I eliminated the idea of a female Ripper since no woman could possess the physical attributes required. This last point is backed up by firm evidence since it seems that on more than one occasion the Ripper approached his victim from behind, clasped his hand over her mouth in order to prevent a scream emerging, pulled back her head thus exposing her neck and slit her throat or strangled her, depending upon the circumstances. To do this the attacker had to be larger than the victim. It would also explain why the Ripper was not covered with his victim's blood since the blood would spurt away from him on to the victim's clothing. Initially, the killer may have approached from the front to allay any initial fears held by the woman, once he was past he could manoeuvre himself accordingly. Exceptions to this rule are the murders of Eliza Anne Chapman and Mary Kelly where the killer had to strike from the front.

I was next alerted by John Richardson, the son of Amelia Richardson who owned 29 Hanbury Street. John Richardson was another one of those shadowy individuals whose actions seemed wrong, especially as he had been in the rear yard where the body was later found. Not satisfied with informing the police that he was in the yard less than one hour before Annie Chapman's body was found, Richardson told the authorities that he had a knife with him.

John Richardson had entered the rear yard of 29 Hanbury Street using the same entrance/exit point as the killer. His object was to carry out a security check on the cellar doors of the house which were positioned in the rear yard, and which had been the subject of a previous attempted break-in. Amelia Richardson had become paranoid about the doors, and John only carried out the checks to appease her. Richardson told the police that as he walked along the passage leading to the rear yard he felt his boots pinching his feet. Stopping in the doorway leading down into the rear yard, he paused to sit upon the steps, remove his boot and hack the uncomfortable piece of leather from the boot with his knife. It was beside these steps that Annie Chapman's body was to be found, just one hour later.

At the resulting inquest Richardson was questioned at great length by the coroner with particular reference to his knife. The coroner told Richardson to return home and bring the knife to court for examination. Unfortunately there is no further mention of this knife and one must presume that it was of a different sort to that used by the killer. It seems that from this point in time Richardson was officially cleared from any further involvement in the enquiry.

It should be remembered that the police located a water-soaked leather apron in the rear yard of Hanbury Street which was later identified as belonging to John Richardson. I am convinced that it would take little to portray him as 'Leather Apron' himself! However, to do so would be unfair and incorrect since John Richardson can be completely exonerated from the enquiry as nothing further is known about him. Certainly the police were not suspicious of him, so there is no reason for anyone else to be so. Without doubt he is an innocent man.

Two suspects gone, and both had seemed quite reasonable. I was beginning to feel that my research would reveal little. However, I was totally convinced that the Ripper was a local man, and that the police of the time might well have overlooked some minor clue which would be crucial to the whole affair. It was to be some considerable time before I came upon another individual who aroused my suspicions, but my next choice was to be final as suddenly fact after fact fell into place as in a jigsaw. The mysterious veil of doubt and suspicion began to lift. Amazingly, my suspect appeared to have positioned himself in the firing-line over the years, but for reasons best left undisclosed had not been recognized as a serious suspect.

The killer had to possess the ability to blend into insignificance and mix with average East End people who would see him going to and coming from his crimes, yet he must never once arouse suspicion. He also had to be able to read and write. Such persons were in abundance in the East End, but not in the area with which we are concerned.

On 23 December 1860, a second son to Maria and David Barnett was born. His name was Joseph though whether this had any bearing upon the time of year at which he was born or not I cannot determine. His parents were devout Roman Catholics. They had arrived in the East End in the 1850s and resided at 127 Middlesex Street where Joseph was born. This house was close to the epicentre of the Ripper murders.

David Barnett was a general dealer who rented barrows in Whitechapel Road and Middlesex Street markets. A hard working man, he worked long hard hours to maintain a reasonable lifestyle for his family, slightly above the poverty line, but in no way secure. Maria Barnett (formerly Lazarus) was also a hard worker who would spend her days repairing trousers and other items of clothing, while looking after the children. Young Joseph attended a number of different schools in the East End and was a bright boy. However, the economics of the Barnett family's situation dictated that Joseph would often miss school to assist his father on the market stall. As he grew, he would roam the grimy streets with other children trying to raise money for his family by any form open to him, be it beg, steal or borrow. The majority of children in this area were forced to find work in order to ease their family's burden, and with next to no work available, the children resorted to other means of procuring goods. Joseph was no different to these children, although life must have been somewhat easier since his father had regular employment.

As the years passed, Joseph grew into an astute young man, though his parents sheltered him from the evil ways of life in Whitechapel/Spitalfields, and allowed him every opportunity to read and write and progress academically. Yet, it has to be said that the young Joseph Barnett must have gained a certain amount of cunning guile from his adolescence and the street law of the district. Like his father, Joseph had principles; his main objective seems to have been to escape from the cesspit of the Victorian East End, and to begin life afresh in a cleaner part of England. In 1883 he found employment at a clerical grade with an agricultural company outside Leicester. Mysteriously, he returned to his home in the East End within months of his departure, though this may be accounted for by the fact that his mother had taken ill, and his father, who had died some time previously, may have bred into Joseph the notion that once he was gone, it was Joseph's responsibility to take care of his mother. Following in his father's footsteps, Barnett soon found work as a labourer and porter in the giant Spitalfields fruit market. Maria Barnett returned to her husband's home country of Ireland, leaving Joseph to fend for himself in London. Initially he seemed to do quite well and took regular lodgings in a house in George Street. Slowly, he became a recluse with no liking for alcohol or social activities. The activities of prostitutes in the area may well have disgusted Barnett who saw the women as a public nuisance, accosting every man who walked past them on the streets. Not one of these harridans was in the image of his mother, none of them wanted the responsibility of a family. Joseph Barnett knew that he was approaching the age when he should settle down with a nice wife and raise a family much in the way that his parents had raised him. Yet, how could he find his ideal woman among the dirty whores of Victorian Whitechapel? Back in Ireland, Maria Barnett passed away, an incident which caused Joseph much grief. For a long time, he could not forget the love he felt for his mother, and his eagerness to settle down became more urgent. Joseph needed to be loved and to love.

By 1884 he had gained employment as a fish-porter in Billingsgate fish market. The job involved collecting fish from the side of the Thames and cleaning and gutting them. It was a skilled job, since it was not easy to gut and clean the fish without damaging or bruising them, as any evident damage would make them unsellable. Barnett and his fellow porters were expected to prepare up to 200 fish per day minimum. For some unknown reason, Barnett was released from his work at the fish market in December 1887. From information I have received from present-day fish-porters, it seems that the only reasons for dismissal would be due to poor workload or suspicion of theft or other breach of local regulations. I do not know why Barnett was dismissed, but it seems unlikely that his workload would have suffered after working at the establishment for almost four years, so he may well have committed a minor breach of the strict regulations. Not to be beaten, Barnett returned to his Spitalfields lodgings where he summoned up his resilience and resources and managed to gain employment in the area's other market that of Spitalfields' fruit and vegetable. The work was somewhat irregular, but at least it provided some form of income for the introvert Irish cockney. At one stage he was able to work on a part-time basis back at Billingsgate, possibly assisting a colleague who was desperate for assistance. It is somewhat remarkable that during the Ripper enquiry, many of the national newspapers revealed that Joseph Barnett was known at the fish market as 'Jack' and others christened him 'John'. A common nickname for John is often Jack, hence the different names in the press. It appears that Barnett preferred John to his true name; for what reason I do not know, but there is obviously some reasoning in his preference. I looked into the fact that he might have worked near to another Joseph, but it may just be that the name may have been so common to use it would cause complications within the market.

Barnett moved around the lodging-houses of the district with alarming frequency. He seems to have favoured 'Macs' in Little George Street, off the Minories; the true identity of the owner and the house number are now unknown. Barnett's other regular haunts included George Street, Thrawl Street and occasionally Brick Lane, with the latter being a last resort. At twenty-six years of age, Joseph Barnett was an insecure young man. His father had settled down by that age, his brother was an established family man, yet Barnett found so many problems with each of the women he looked at. Many of the working men he knew lived with women of the street and spoke of the problems encountered through such relationships. The main problem was that the average Victorian East End male had no respect for women whatsoever and would regularly physically and verbally abuse his mate. These facts caused Barnett to remain aloof of the women of the street and to maintain his interest in improving his life in general. He knew that some day he would meet the woman who could be his replacement mother figure.

On Friday 8 April 1887, an incident took place which was to alter Joseph Barnett's life so dramatically that it is doubtful that he would have become involved had he known the eventual outcome. *En route* to his Thrawl Street lodgings, Barnett met with a prostitute in Commercial Street who approached him in the usual way. Barnett fell for the girl instantly who vividly reminded him of his late mother, her plump good looks and soft Irish brogue led Barnett to ask her for a drink. Because of his upbringing and principles, it is almost certain that Barnett would have prized his new acquaintance so highly that no sexual encounter would have taken place on this initial meeting. The thought may well have crossed his mind that he should find out as much as he could about the woman's background to see if she met with his criteria for a responsible partner. There was obviously some attraction between the two as they arranged to meet the following day, and once this rendezvous had been accomplished the pair decided to live together. The whore was none other than Mary Jane Kelly. It is probable that Barnett would have offered Kelly the world in return for her affection, yet it appears that Barnett himself was the naîve partner as there is evidence which tends to point to Mary Kelly using him.

Despite her age, Mary Jane Kelly was worldly wise and knew the law of survival on the streets. Feminine intuition would have led her to realize that Barnett was taken in by her; in order to impress him, she may have related tales of visits to France with gentlemen, and of a failed relationship with a miner which had ended because of his untimely death. All of this would have indicated to Barnett that here was a woman who wanted to settle down, a woman who was something of a prize since she had been loved by gentlemen. None of the tales were true, of course, they were told to impress a young man who was ready to tell some simple untruths himself concerning his secure employment and financial background. Kelly wanted Barnett for his money and because he could provide a roof over her head; Barnett wanted Kelly because he needed to love someone; and so the relationship commenced on an unstable foundation of lies and untruths.

The couple took lodgings at Whittlowes in George Street, a lodging-house which Barnett had frequented regularly in preceding months. Barnett persuaded Kelly to refrain from prostitution, explaining his ideals and the life he had planned for her as his partner. In consequence, only one wage was coming into the home. Soon simple economics forced the couple to move. Kelly slowly influenced Barnett and introduced him to a new and more sordid lifestyle, the money did not last too long. Barnett and his new partner began to frequent many of the local public houses. He found himself mixing with the women of the street whom he had previously despised; without being aware of it, hopelessly lost in love and passion, Joseph Barnett was being dragged into the pit of human filth and degradation he had fought so hard to avoid. From Whittlowes the couple moved to Paternoster Row, a small court off Dorset Street which lay deep in the heart of slumland. With money so scarce, Barnett resolved to work all the hours he could in order to provide for Mary Kelly and her needs, he knew that by doing so he would be able to keep her off the streets and thus maintain her loyalty and attention towards him. However, what Barnett had failed to recognize was that his loved one did not possess his ideals and principles. While Barnett worked, his lover maintained a steady income for herself through prostitution; her only problem was to ensure that she was home when Barnett returned from his work. But Barnett was slightly more streetwise than his lover gave him credit, he soon realized that she had returned to prostitution. In order to stop this, he regularly failed to attend work so that he could supervise Kelly's whereabouts and prevent her from walking the streets touting for business.

The couple were regulars of the Ten Bells public house on the corner of Fournier Street and Commercial Street, and also of the Britannia on the corner of Dorset Street. Barnett's interest in Kelly had now reached the point of obsession, any income he earned was wasted upon her, and her irresponsible behaviour soon ensured mounting debts. The landlord of their rooms in Paternoster Court came round early one morning to demand his overdue rent, to his shock he found both Barnett and Kelly so drunk that they displayed no apparent concern at the fact that he was throwing them out on to the streets. To be ejected from lodgings in Dorset Street was the ultimate humiliation, even the homeless could usually manage to pay the cheap rent required for rooms in this area, only the dregs of the human race and society would be thrown on to the streets. What had happened to Joseph Barnett's ideals? From the slum surroundings of Dorset Street the couple moved to the notorious Brick Lane no more than two minutes walk away and running more or less parallel with Commercial Street.

These recent events made a deep and lasting impression upon Barnett, resulting in a complete reassessment of his predicament and an attempt to resurrect his life. Since the majority of the problems were of a financial nature, Barnett resumed his arduous hours at the local fish and fruit markets; yet he chose to ignore the fact that his real problem was Mary Kelly. He kept on believing that Kelly was good for him, and would one day be his, to pretend that the competition of punters looking for cheap thrills was non-existent. If only, at this point in time, Barnett had realized that Mary Kelly was no better, and possibly worse, than the middle-aged hags who regularly walked the streets of Whitechapel and Spitalfields, he might well have saved himself much emotional trauma and have escaped the impending crisis.

With Barnett once again working long hours, Kelly maintained her deceitful ways and resumed prostitution, developing many secret relationships with local men. The fact that she kept such affairs a secret from Barnett demonstrates the fact that she was aware that he was obsessed with her. She knew that if he were to find out, it would result in another confrontation, a situation which she wished to avoid since Barnett still gave her everything she wanted and was obsessed with her. Mary Kelly was seen touting for business in many areas and bars, including the Frying Pan in Brick Lane. She established a regular patch on which to whore in Leman Street. This, it seems, served its purpose well as Joseph Barnett had no cause to go near this area on his way to or from his places of work. She could whore until her heart was content, and without Barnett's knowing of it.

The weeks which followed were troublesome as the couple argued regularly. Barnett often returned home to find Kelly missing. His suspicions raised, he would search the pubs and streets for her. Barnett decided once again that it was time to move, so they took rooms in George Yard Buildings, off Wentworth Street and Whitechapel High Street, later they moved to Millers Court (McCarthy's rents) off Dorset Street. By the time the couple moved to Millers Court, Joseph Barnett fully believed that he was in total control of the relationship with Mary Kelly – nothing could have been further from the truth. Whilst settling into 13 Millers Court (and since they had lived in the area for some time mixing and meeting with other prostitutes), the couple must have became acquainted with Mary Ann Nichols, Eliza Annie Chapman, Liz Stride and Catharine Eddowes who had all lived in the same street, drunk in the same taverns and walked the same streets. It was a close-knit community; as indicated by Mrs Caroline Maxwell who informed the coroner at Mary Kelly's inquest that lodging-house people became familiar quickly. Many of these prostitutes were known as local characters to one and all. It is unlikely that the occupants of 13 Millers Court were so immersed in their own tiny world that they did not know fellow residents of local doss-houses, or who drink in the pubs they drank in. Each prostitute would have been aware of the other's existence, it is too much of a coincidence that at least two of them used the alias of Mary or Kelly.

In June 1888, Joseph Barnett became fully aware of his loved one's promiscuity; his mind was sent into spiralling turmoil, his good intentions and attention had been scorned by his partner. His patience was at breaking point, and he was often heard to order Kelly to refrain from prostitution. The deceit and mistrust of their relationship was causing him much grief, but he resolutely determined that he would fight her sexual proclivities and win her over. At the same time, Mary Kelly had decided the opposite, Joseph Barnett had served his useful purpose, and she now wished to terminate their friendship in as gentle a way as possible. Even she realized that it would be in no one's best interest to end the relationship with a blazing argument. Her first priority was to locate either a new partner or new lodgings.

Continuing her ways, Mary Kelly often failed to return to Millers Court leaving Joseph to fret over her whereabouts. She realized that it would be foolish to take a client back to Millers Court since there would be a needless and unnecessary confrontation if Barnett suddenly returned. Barnett's frame of mind began to alter, he despised Kelly's prostitute friends, blaming them for Kelly's reluctance to commit herself to a full relationship with him and encouraging her into a life of prostitution. In an attempt to resolve matters as best he could, Barnett resolved to work hard so that he could shower Kelly with gifts and cash. Kelly unhesitatingly accepted Barnett's generosity and wasted his hard-earned money upon drink and clients and fellow prostitutes. Then, without warning, Barnett was once again released from employment, this time it was much harder to bear because of his emotional problems. July 1888 saw him sink lower than ever before and this time no escape route was evident. The shame of being unemployed again was more than Barnett's insecure psychological state of mind could accept; with no job, he had no money or anything else to offer Kelly, deep in his own heart he knew that the relationship was over, but he refused to accept his fate.

Today, the pressures of unemployment and the loss of status as the main earner often causes the male head of the household much in the way of psychological problems. Chiefly, of course, the ego is dented, but further problems are created over time with increasing debts and a feeling of rejection. It is a recorded fact that most cases of wife-beating occur during moments of economic crisis and times of distress. The pressures force normal individuals in to commit silly crimes so that they can feel in control of the situation and recover the feeling of being the family's provider. The pressures placed upon Joseph Barnett were no different to those endured today, along with his financial and employment problems was the fact that he was suffering systematic psychological punishment from his loved one who chose to ignore him and did not respect him. It was perhaps this last which hurt him more than all the rest. His mother and father had had the greatest respect for each other, yet he could not command anything from his partner. Joseph Barnett was a survivor, he knew something would ease his situation, but what and when it would be he could not guess.

The early morning editions of the local and national press of 8 August 1888 ran a story of murder in Whitechapel. Joseph Barnett read to Mary Kelly an account of how a prostitute had been found stabbed to death in George Yard Buildings. The woman had been identified as Martha Tabram/Turner. The columns concerning the crime gave much detail as to how it had been committed. To his surprise, Mary Kelly seemed to be genuinely shocked by the affair and in fear of the attacker who had so far escaped police detection. Barnett revelled in the gruesome details and talked of the crime with much enthusiasm. The couple must have spoken of how they had once resided at George Yard Buildings, and talked about Tabram/Turner as a local prostitute. The whole area of Whitechapel/Spitalfields was shocked by the murder, their fears were aroused by the fact that the press claimed the killer must be some kind of maniac since the body had been stabbed thirty-nine times. Like other prostitutes, Mary Kelly became reluctant to venture out alone at night, and Barnett's cautions on the perils of prostitution seemed to have some impact on her since she elected to keep off the streets for a short while.

At last, Joseph Barnett had been provided with a solution to his problem. If he kept reminding Kelly of the murder in George Yard Buildings it might cause her to renounce prostitution as a way of life, and to remain with him. But time is a great healer, and slowly life in Whitechapel/Spitalfields returned to normal as the murder of Martha Tabram/Turner slipped from memory. Once more Mary Kelly was actively involved in prostitution. Barnett could find no suitable employment anywhere and had become aggressive towards Kelly. The rent arrears of the tiny room which the couple shared increased at a rate of four shillings per week. With these worries constantly running through his mind, Joseph Barnett was forced to take some kind of action, that it was not correct was certainly the result of erratic judgement caused by his mental state of mind. Realizing that his verbal intimidation of Mary Kelly had failed, he resolved to hunt down each of Kelly's prostitute friends individually. These individuals were specially selected so that their deaths would have as much impact upon Kelly as possible, and would drive her back into his arms. The image and name of Jack the Ripper were created to instil fear into a particular social class of people, prostitutes, and, in particular, Mary Kelly. The mutilations were carried out to ensure that the crimes were given headline publicity by the press.

For a while, Barnett's plan went as planned, until 28 October 1888 when Mary Kelly (who perhaps had cause to suspect Barnett, especially as he seemed obsessed by the crimes) invited a fellow prostitute to live with her in her room at 13 Millers Court. Joseph Barnett had no idea that Kelly had done this and, once he was aware, refused to give his consent, but Kelly would not change her mind. Barnett suffered the inconvenience for two nights before the inevitable quarrel between the couple took place. At some stage during the fracas which followed a window was broken, and eventually the violence ended. Mary Kelly used her tongue to inflict a verbal barrage of insults against Barnett and requested that he leave at once. Barnett had no alternative, the affair was over, begrudgingly he gathered together his meagre possessions and walked from Millers Court to take lodgings with Mr Buller at 24–25 New Street.

It is incumbent to add that during the quarrel between the couple which took place on 30 October 1888, Mary Kelly must have asked Barnett for the door key to the room. He said he was unable to return it since it had been lost, in his mind this refusal ensured that Kelly could not lock him from the room if he wished to return. Whether the key was lost or not is of no direct consequence, but what is certain is that Kelly asked him how she was to secure the room now that the key was missing. Barnett showed Kelly how she could put her hand through the broken window and slip the sliding catch into the locked position, to all intents and purposes the door would be barred against anyone who tried it from outside. Mary Kelly accepted the solution, and Barnett left, with much anger inside him. The problem begins when one realizes that when the body of Mary Kelly was found on that damp November morning of 1888 the door to the room had been locked with a key and by use of the sliding bolt. Therefore, the killer of Mary Kelly had been in possession of the key which Barnett claimed he had lost. Not only that, but he had also known the secret of sliding the bolt using the broken window for access. The number of people who would have known of this technique can be greatly reduced when one remembers that Kelly never took unknown clients back to her room, especially after Barnett had read from newspapers the varied descriptions of the killer. Kelly was frightened of meeting the killer and would not have taken unnecessary risks.

The first person arrested after the Mary Kelly murder was none other than Joseph Barnett. This took place after the 'Ripper Squad' had been on the scene for several minutes and had assessed the crime as another Ripper killing. Had they suspected anyone else of being the Ripper, they would not have arrested Barnett. It is true that in most cases of murder the killer is known to the victim, but the fact that they arrested Barnett suggests they thought he was the Ripper. No amount of speculation can deny the fact that he was arrested and held at Millers Court by the Ripper squad. Further suspicion against Barnett is raised when one considers whether he would have told the police they could gain entry to the room by using the sliding bolt. He must have told them this since Inspector Abberline knew of it at the inquest. This shows that the door must have been locked with a key, and if Barnett provided that, he would have blown his cover, the key was missing for he had thrown the key away before it could be found on him. The fact that the door had been locked with a key is further corroborated by the fact that a contemporary sketch exists depicting the police forcing open the door with a pickaxe. After identifying the remains of Mary Kelly, Barnett was taken to Commercial Street police station where he was questioned by Inspector Abberline, and the following statement was recorded:

> Statement of Joseph Barnett, 9 November 1888, now residing at 24-25 New Street, Bishopsgate. (a common lodging house)
> I am a porter in Billingsgate Market, but have been out of employment for the past three to four months. I have been living with Marie Jeanette Kelly who occupied number 13 room, Millers Court. I have lived with her altogether about 18 months, for the last 8 months in Millers Court, until last Tuesday week (30 ulto) when in consequence of not earning sufficient money to give her and her resorting to prostitution, I resolved on leaving her, but I was friendly with her and called to see her between seven and eight p.m. Thursday (8th) and told her I was very sorry I had no work and that I could not give her any money. I left her about 8 o'clock same evening and that was the last time I saw her alive.
>
> There was a woman in the room when I called. The deceased told me on one occasion that her father, named John Kelly was a foreman of some Iron Works and lived at Carmarthen or Caernarvon, that she had a brother named Henry serving in the 2nd batallion Scots Guards and known amongst his colleagues as John too, and I believe the regiment is now in Ireland. She told me that she had obtained her livelihood as a prostitute for some considerable time before I took her from the streets, and that she left her home about four years ago, and that she was married to a collier who was killed through some explosion. I think she said her husband's name was Davis or Davies.

The above statement displays some insight into how Barnett saw his relationship with Kelly, as well as providing some weak alibis. 'She told me that she obtained her livelihood as a prostitute for some considerable time before I took her from the streets.' This sounds as though he was on some kind of crusade, taking her off the streets, it also displays his dislike of the prostitute class. Why should he apologize to her for having no money and no work? And why did he wait nine days before returning to do so? It is more likely that he returned on the off chance of catching her alone, was shocked and surprised to see another prostitute there, and therefore decided to appear to remain on friendly terms. They most certainly were not on such terms on the night of 30 October 1888.

My next point concerns Barnett's reasons for leaving Kelly which seem to alter dramatically almost overnight. Initially, he told Inspector Abberline that he had left her because he was not earning sufficient money to give her, and she had resorted to prostitution. Yet, at the inquest, his reply to the identical question is, 'Because she had a woman of bad character there, whom she took out of compassion, and I objected to it. That was the only reason'. Altering vital statements like this should have resulted in a detailed inquest, but as we know this never transpired. I fail to see how Barnett could have altered his reason for leaving in the space of three days; the truth would have stuck firmly in his mind, but untruths tend to alter. During police questioning, Barnett was asked what he was doing on the night of the murder and informed the authorities that he was playing whist at Bullers lodging-house, in New Street until 12.30 a.m. when he retired to bed. There is no evidence to disprove this, but likewise there is no corroborating evidence to support it. New Street is some four minutes walk from Millers Court, access in 1888 was via back alleys off Sandy Row and through Raven Row and Crispin Street which leads directly on to Dorset Street. Assisted by poor illumination, Barnett would have been perfectly situated to commit the Dorset Street murder. By playing whist, Barnett had created the ideal alibi for himself, especially when he made a great deal of going to bed shortly after midnight. Playing whist was not his normal form of social activity and one wonders why he suddenly took it up – unless it was done for a specific purpose.

The next factor to take into consideration comes from the statement made by George Hutchinson. Though I dismiss much of this testimony as rubbish, there is a chance that it is loosely based upon fact. Hutchinson claimed that when he spoke to Kelly on the morning of her death, she told him she intended to earn as much money as she could in order to clear her rent arrears. Yet the police surgeon who examined the body in Millers Court estimated the time of death as being around 2 or 3 a.m., he also stated that she had been murdered whilst lying on the right side of her bed. Bearing in mind the fact that all of her clothes had been neatly folded upon a chair, it is obvious that she had finished her street-walking for that night/morning and had gone to bed, possibly with a client who had been lying on the left side of the bed. What had caused the sudden change in her plans? At one moment she was telling a friend that she was desperate for money and intended to work all night if need-be, the next moment she had gone to bed with a client for the evening. It must be added that Kelly never took her clients back to her room, through fear of the Ripper and of Barnett, yet we are told that she entertained two separate males in her room that morning, one of whom was intent upon staying throughout the rest of the hours of darkness. The solution to these anomalies is that Mary Kelly must have known the individual she took back to her room that morning. She was too frightened and too intelligent to risk taking a man who resembled the Ripper back to her room, however, if her suspicion was allayed, she may have been fooled into allowing a familiar face in. Considering that Barnett had not visited Kelly for almost nine days, one must ask why he should suddenly turn up the night before her death, and why his pipe was found on the mantelpiece in the room on the morning of her death. The answer is that although he had returned to 13 Millers Court to ask Kelly to take him back, the presence of the other prostitute had caused him to defer any suggestion until she had left. If Kelly had denied him again, Barnett could have left, returning to his lodgings to plan his return. However, Kelly would not have feared Barnett too much, and would perhaps have condescended to allow him one last night of pleasure, for a small fee. This would explain a great deal: why she lay on the right side of the bed, why his pipe was found in the room and why she felt so relaxed that she had folded her clothes upon the chair. Furthermore, if anyone saw Barnett in the room it would have aroused no suspicion, thus leaving him free to kill her. His sudden appearance shortly before her death and the presence of his pipe in the room are tantalizingly important, and too much of an obvious conclusion to be a coincidence. This is all evidence which points in one direction and cannot be overlooked or dismissed as trivia. It is direct evidence which links the killer with the victim; never before has anyone been able to link a suspect in this way.

The day following Barnett's release from police custody, he was tracked down by an enthusiastic reporter to a public house in Bishopsgate. During the interview which followed, and in subsequent press interviews, Barnett's phraseology left much to be desired. When speaking of Mary Kelly he continually refers to her as 'the deceased' and displays little or no sympathy, indeed he tends to verge on arrogance rather than remorse. Here is a different side to Barnett's character: the love of his life has been butchered by Jack the Ripper and he sits calmly in a public house drinking and apparently unperturbed by the situation. A man whose upbringing was full of principles and responsibilities suddenly changes his ways and displays an *alter ego* which is blasé towards other people's emotions. It is as if Barnett wanted to escape from what was occurring around him; his mind had switched off refusing to accept responsibility for his actions. He realized that he could not leave London, nor run away, as this would again arouse suspicion. When speaking to reporters, he would say that he often gave Kelly money, but failed to say why. This is a classic display of caution, as Barnett attempts to throw the blame on to Kelly and muster pity for himself, but his actions and words defied all logical explanation. These were not the actions of a shocked lover in mourning, but of a man who wanted a breathing space, until now up to date the Ripper had managed to remain anonymous, but now he had exposed himself and his personal relationship with the victim had caused a sensation around him.

The author of the legendary Jack the Ripper letters, claimed to have kept some of the victims' blood in ginger-beer bottles and said it had gone thick like glue. Although there is much speculation about the authenticity of these letters found within Mary Kelly's room, the very room which Joseph Barnett had once occupied, were a number of ginger-beer bottles. Could these be those self-same bottles identified within the mocking Ripper letters? Is this a piece of evidence which directly links Barnett with a part of the police investigation? The ginger beer bottle theory is rather weak as such bottles were to be found in abundance all over the metropolis, but it still causes a closer inspection of Barnett's role in the killings. Continuing with the Ripper letters, the phrasing contained within these is directed towards prostitutes, and was penned by someone who disliked them, 'I am down on whores' and 'shan't quit ripping till I do get buckled', are remarks made to instil fear and this fits in directly with Barnett's motives. Add to this the fact that Barnett regularly read the newspaper articles on the murders to Kelly and one can begin to piece together the final pieces of the jigsaw. From the police files and other such evidence we have evidence that Joseph Barnett could read and write, though unfortunately I have been unable to procure any samples of his handwriting, if any exist, so cannot compare them with the handwriting of the Ripper letters.

On the night of 30 September 1888, Jack the Ripper struck twice, once in Berner Street and again in Mitre Square. It is generally assumed that he failed to satiate his appetite for blood because he had not mutilated Liz Stride in that yard off Berner Street. I disagree with this assumption. There is little in the way of evidence which links the Stride murder with those of Jack the Ripper, other than flimsy sightings of a number of suspicious individuals carrying parcels in their left hands or with a woman fitting the description of Liz Stride. Indeed one such account came from a man who was nothing more than a sensationalist and was later to claim he had been visited by American police who were alleged to have informed him of secret information in relation to the crimes. We know that murder was a common occurrence in both Whitechapel and Spitalfields during this era, and also that the most common form was cut-throat murder by use of a knife. Who is to say that Stride was not murdered by a different hand for a different reason such as robbery? The Berner Street murder took place at probably the most distant of all the murder sites and would have entailed much more walking and hiding than any of the other murders which were committed closer to the Commercial Street area. Alternatively, if we assume that Stride was also a victim, it means that there must be some explanation for the killer not mutilating her and then venturing into Mitre Square. Perhaps, if the Ripper did kill Liz Stride, he was disturbed by the return of the club steward on his horse and cart and had insufficient time to commit any mutilations. Fleeing the scene, he calmly walked on to Mitre Square, with his appetite for blood forcing him on, there he met with Catharine Eddowes, and the rest is history. I question whether he continued to Mitre Square, a bloodthirsty animal could not have walked such a distance in a calm manner, he would have been agitated and excited. However, consider that a calm man who had been defeated in his purpose through being disturbed by some person walks away from Berner Street, not with the purpose of satiating his bloodthirsty appetite, but because he knows that he must mutilate to maintain the sensational aspect of his crimes (after all, a simple throat-cutting job would hardly make headlines, but another Ripper mutilation would) and frighten Mary Kelly off the streets and back into his arms. In either circumstance, I honestly believe that the Stride attack was a coincidence, but I am possibly alone in thinking this. I must confess that the presence of the murder in the police file seems to dictate that evidence at the time led police to believe that it was a Ripper job, but examination of the papers reveals little or nothing other than the fact that a similar murder technique was employed. This may have been a copy-cat attack and with little evidence available I remain dubious whether this was a Ripper killing.

The police claimed that they positively sighted the Ripper as he left Mitre Square, seconds after committing the crime. Detective Stephen White revealed the following:

> For five nights we had been watching a certain alley just behind Whitechapel Road. It could only be entered from where we had two men posted in hiding, and persons entering the alley were under observation by the two men. It was a bitter cold night when I arrived at the scene to take the report of the two men in hiding. I was turning away when I saw a man coming out of the alley. He was walking quickly but noiselessly, apparently wearing rubber shoes, which were rather rare in those days. I stood aside to let the man pass, and as he came under the wall lamp I got a good look at him. He was about five feet ten inches in height, and was dressed rather shabbily, though it was obvious that the material of his clothes was good. Evidently a man who had seen better days, I thought, but men who have seen better days are common enough down East, and that in itself was not sufficient to justify me stopping him. His face was long and thin, nostrils rather delicate and his hair was jet black. His complexion was inclined to be sallow, and altogether the man was foreign in appearance. The most striking thing about him, however, was the extraordinary brilliance of his eyes. They looked like two very luminous glow worms coming through the darkness. The man was slightly bent at the shoulders, though he was obviously quite young – about 33 at the most and gave one the idea of having been a student or professional man. His hands were snow white and the fingers long and tapering.

White continues, recalling how he spoke to the man who had bid him 'Goodnight' and how, just moments later, a mutilated body was discovered in the alley. The keen detective tells how he set off in pursuance of the stranger but lost him within the labyrinth of back alleys and lanes. This report is quite incredible, in as much as it was not released for some time after the affair, yet displays excellent descriptive passages. Though the precise murder site has not been accurately defined, it is presumed to be Mitre Square, as none of the other sites fit the description as closely. White claims that rubber shoes were quite rare in those days which tends to suggest that the whole affair has been conjured up. In fact, rubber shoes were quite easily obtained, detectives were issued with them, as too were the special patrols organized by the Whitechapel Vigilance Committee. White's declaration is not all that it seems. The description of the man seen by White is identical to that of Joseph Barnett – and very probably half a million other persons – and contemporary sketches picture Barnett in much the same manner as described by Detective White.

There is evidence to prove that after killing Catharine Eddowes in Mitre Square, the Ripper headed north, eventually arriving in a court off Dorset Street where it is claimed that he washed the blood from his hands. The various street and sewer maps I have examined display few public sinks, and indeed one of the few in the immediate area of Dorset Street is within Millers Court. This displays a good geographical knowledge of the area, it also depicts an individual who dared to enter the inner confines of the roughest community in the East End, therefore the killer was a local man who would not look out of place in Dorset Street or even Millers Court. As we are aware, Joseph Barnett resided within Millers Court at the time of the Eddowes murder, the blood in the sink may well have been that of Eddowes washed from Barnett's hands prior to him walking into number 13 to greet Mary Kelly and allay her suspicions. The route to Dorset Street from Mitre Square would have taken Barnett along Goulston Street where he could deposit the piece of apron covered in faecal matter in the doorway of Wentworth Dwellings.

There is much in the way of descriptions from alleged witnesses which give us a picture of the alleged killer; all depict him as being in his mid to late twenties or possibly early thirties, with a moustache and of similar build, all describe him as being of a smart and respectable appearance. It is no coincidence that at the inquest of Mary Kelly, Doctor R. MacDonald commented upon Joseph Barnett's respectable appearance. It is also a curious comment for a coroner to make and perhaps was made for the benefit of the police and other authorities, as a kind of acknowledgement of their possible suspicions. The inquest of Mary Kelly was alarmingly short. The real reason behind this has never been released, but it may well be that the authorities had suspicions about Barnett and did not wish to alert him to this so that much of the information was deliberately withheld. This allowed the police to continue their surveillance of Barnett.

It appears that this quiet, unassuming Irish cockney who drifts in and out of the whole saga with regularity has fooled an entire nation for over one hundred years. Each of the personality and psychological traits which apply to latter and present day mass murderers appears in Joseph Barnett. The similarities between his crimes and those of Peter Sutcliffe, the 'Yorkshire Ripper', are unbelievable. Both men hunted down prostitutes and committed horrendous acts on their bodies. Sutcliffe, like Barnett, lived within the district where the crimes took place and was interviewed on several occasions by police-officers. The only difference between the two lies in their actual motive for killing.

Once Joseph Barnett accepted that his crimes were only a temporary solution to his problems, he realized that the end had to be close. The final fuse was ignited by Kelly when she ejected him from the love-nest and declared that their relationship was over. Being astute, he realized that an immediate response to Kelly's attack would be incriminating, so he composed himself and managed to restrain his actions until he visited Kelly on the night of 8 November 1888 when once again his anger within was ignited. Returning late in the evening of that same night or perhaps in the early hours of the following morning, Barnett, alone with Kelly, could commit murder and mutilate her until his heart was content. The rejection he felt caused him to hate Mary Kelly and to destroy her. If he could not have her, then he intended to make sure that every man who saw her after her death would feel nothing but repulsion and reject the possibility that she was attractive. The gross mutilations and the stripping of the skin from her face display Barnett's yearning for immortal power and control over Kelly; all those months when he had been submissive to her disappeared through the blade of his knife; and so Mary Kelly was no more, and Jack the Ripper disappeared into obscurity.

Many people may be of the opinion that a killer such as the Ripper simply could not stop killing. I do not accept this. Barnett's whole rationale for murder was to force a woman into his arms and to reform her character. Once this objective had failed, he had no further reason to kill. The legal records of this country, indeed the world, are full of murderers who killed on numerous occasions and escaped detection. Even mass killers will often lead otherwise normal lives until they are arrested to the surprise of everyone from their families and closest friends to acquaintances. Because the Ripper mutilated his victims, it has been decreed that he must have been insane. This is not so. Mass murderer Peter Manuel once committed a burglary in Scotland. Once the robbery was complete and knowing full well that he had escaped detection, he returned to the house and butchered the sleeping family of four by blowing out their brains from close range with a shotgun. There was no reason for murder and one would conclude that Manuel was an insensitive animal with no feeling for life. Not so, for having murdered the sleeping family, he ventured into the living area of the house and saw a kitten wandering around. Feeling sorry for the kitten, he gently stroked it and gave it a bowl of milk before making his escape. Like Joseph Barnett, Peter Manuel was capable of committing violent acts one moment, and sympathetic loving actions the next.

Murder is irrational, that precise moment when emotions take over actions may last just a few seconds, but allow sufficient time to destroy another. Murder can be committed and forgotten with no real lasting mental or psychological problems. It is quite feasible that if Dennis Nilsen or Peter Sutcliffe had not been caught through genuine mistakes, they would have escaped detection and eventually overcome their problems.

It is a well documented fact that the majority of authorities believed Jack the Ripper possessed some kind of anatomical skill or medical knowledge. Once again I disagree. It is claimed that in the Mitre Square murder the killer removed a piece of his victim's apron, in order to wipe the blood from his hands. In truth, different evidence shows that the killer had in fact severed the victim's anal artery thus sending faecal matter spewing out onto his hands and knife. The piece of apron was being removed so that he could wipe human excreta from his hands and knife, not blood. Such actions do not indicate the articulate hand of a person with medical knowledge, nor are they the operations of a doctor or a surgeon. Indeed in 1888, Doctor D.G. Halstead of the London Hospital believed that the skills used in the mutilations could have been acquired by a man accustomed to boning and filleting fish. Need I remind you of Joseph Barnett's occupation?

On Saturday 10 November 1888, Joseph Barnett was ejected from Bullers lodgings in New Street. The landlord decided that he would prefer Barnett to leave, as he had become a nuisance with his continual teasing of the press since the Kelly murder. From New Street, he moved to 21 Portpool Lane where he lived with his sister. Eventually, Barnett returned to a life of markets and labouring jobs. Like so many other East-enders, Barnett came to forget the crimes of Jack the Ripper, but it was a few years before he began to make anything of his life. He managed to purchase his own fruit stall, and met a local woman, whom I only know by her pet name 'Goldie'. There is no record of the couple marrying, but a son was born of the relationship. The relationship with 'Goldie' failed to stand the test of time. Thereafter, Barnett led a quiet sheltered life, preferring to remain aloof of the legendary Whitechapel murders. He rented property in Old Ford Road, Bethnal Green, and it was at this address that he died on 15 March 1927 suffering from 'lympho sarcoma' of the cervical or mesenteric gland, a complaint from which he had suffered for about three years. Certain individuals have asked that his place of burial and the precise address in Old Ford Road at which he died remain anonymous. There is no reason for publishing such data, its release would only affect people presently living or working there. The fact of the matter is that Jack the Ripper is long dead, only his memory lives on.

The case against Joseph Barnett is straightforward and simple, not one of immense complexity as are so many other theories about the Ripper. Murder, like life, is relatively simple, and so too, generally speaking, are the solutions to life's problems. In answer to Joseph Barnett/Jack the Ripper's taunt of 1888, 'Catch Me When You Can', we can now reply, 'Joseph/Jack, it has taken over a century, but we have caught you! Now your ghost may finally be laid to rest.'

6 Strange Meetings

When I initially commenced research into this subject some six years ago, I confess to being somewhat naïve about the Ripper legend and I was intrigued by the suggestions made by authors and members of the public in general. The fact that the name of Jack the Ripper will live for ever more is certain, his legend is known in households all over the world, and thousands visit the sites where he committed his various atrocities. This interest is not unhealthy or morbid, it relies on the simple fact that we all enjoy a good murder. The basic elements of a good murder are mystery, intrigue and violence, and can anyone think of a more mysterious group of crimes than those of Jack the Ripper?

The Whitechapel of today is not as it was when Joseph/Jack walked its dingy cobbled streets. If he were alive today, I doubt whether he would be able to walk from Dorset Street to Hanbury Street since multi-storey car-parks, and modern office blocks fill the district. At this present time just one of the original murder sites still exists, that of Bucks Row, now renamed Durward Street. It is a distinct possibility that, by the time you read this, nothing will remain as the city developers move in and destroy the crumbling dilapidated shells which were once grand Victorian buildings. Despite all this, the East End of London will forever remain synonymous with the crimes of Jack the Ripper. The legend will never die, nor will its fascination cease to intrigue aspiring criminologists and would-be true-crime researchers.

It is then without doubt, that you as a reader and possible expert on the crimes of Jack the Ripper, will wonder just what I am going to reveal in this chapter. Almost every researcher of any standing will expound on certain information which he has uncovered which has never before been released or revealed. This has certainly been the case in many of the works covering the murders of the Ripper. Almost every author can reveal stories of mysterious meetings and strange encounters during his rambles through 'Jack Streets'. I too have had such encounters; yet the two I am about to unfold, are not that mysterious, in fact it may transpire that they are fully bona fide. I have no reason to doubt them, but there are those who are professional cynics and view everything printed in relation to the Ripper as extremely dubious. I do not expect that everyone who reads this work will accept it, that is subject to different opinions and different interpretations on certain evidence as well as, most importantly, access to the required data. I do not wish to create a mystery concerning secret files or anything of that nature, one simply has to research the correct files and identify what one is searching for.

Around three years ago, when I was partway through my research, I received a telephone call from a then London-based chief inspector by the name of Mick Wyatt, a gentleman whom I had never spoken to before. Through the excellent police network he had heard of my research and believed that he had information which might be of assistance to me. He gave me a telephone number and asked me to contact it at my leisure. It was almost three weeks before I got round to ringing the number, and initially it seemed to be another wasted effort for I was advised that, if I was interested, he knew the whereabouts of what had been claimed as a genuine Ripper artifact. With thoughts of another knife for my collection or a bloodstained handkerchief, I asked what he believed he had located? 'It's a shawl,' he replied, 'belonging to one of the victims, but I am not sure about which one.' I asked other questions, including the location of the shawl and was advised that it was in Clacton-on-Sea, Essex. I noted the address and placed it in my file where it remained for a further year or so.

Eventually, late in November 1989, I was able to track down the location of the shawl. It was in a video shop in Clacton, a seaside town not normally known for its Jack the Ripper connection. I rang the shop-owners, John and Janice Dowler, and explained just who I was and what I was doing. Expecting a little animosity, I was surprised to hear the dulcet tones of a Londoner who was only too pleased to assist me in my quest. I arranged an appointment and visited the shop, which is located in St Osyth Road, Clacton. In person, the Dowlers were even more hospitable, and as keen as I to authenticate the shawl. Both were extremely cynical about the shawl's authenticity, and neither was prepared to claim that it was a genuine article. This impressed me as one anticipates false claims when investigating such matters. After interviewing John and Janice, I ascertained that it was allegedly the shawl of Catharine Eddowes, and had been removed from the body either at the scene or *en route* to the morgue. The shawl had come into the couple's possession several years ago when a friend, who knew an antique dealer, offered it to the couple as they hailed from London. Not knowing too much about the Ripper murders, the couple asked to see the shawl first and it was brought round to the shop some days later. The couple both said they felt somewhat emotional about the shawl when they eventually held it. This was not through any mysterious vibes emanating from it, but because of its history. The friend left the shawl with the couple, and a few days later he was invited by the Dowlers to return to collect it as they did not want it in their home. Some days later he returned with framed pieces of the shawl. 'It was obvious when we had the shawl, that a piece was missing,' claimed John; the missing section had, in fact, been framed by the antique dealer and now hangs on the wall on display in the shop. On researching the Eddowes file, I was disappointed to find that there is no mention of a shawl. However, the description of the dress worn by Catharine Eddowes on the night of her death perfectly matches the piece of shawl in the frame: tiny flowered patterns, containing the colours blue, pink, green, yellow and maroon. It is an almost identical description, but since there is no record of Catharine Eddowes owning or possessing a shawl on the night of her death we are left to wonder.

On the rear of the sealed frame containing the pieces of shawl is the inscription, 'Two silk samples, taken from Catharine Eddowes' shawl at the time of the discovery of her body by Amos SIMPSON in 1888. (*End of September*) Victim of Jack the Ripper. Surface printed silk circa 1886'.

The name of the police constable who found Catharine Eddowes was of course Edward Watkins, but a name can easily be misconstrued over a period of time. Certainly no officer of that name served in the City of London Police during that period, so if he actually existed he must have been in the

Metropolitan Force, but I believe that this may be a case of mistaken identity. What is more interesting is the question why, if the shawl was intended to be an elaborate hoax, it has not come to light until now. The originator would, one imagines, have required some form of reward (be it financial or otherwise) for his efforts, yet the fact remains that the shawl's existence and location have never before been released. The piece of shawl which is currently located in Clacton was almost certainly framed prior to any information being released from the police files. Therefore, the person who originated the claims about the shawl must either have had private information relating to the description of Catharine Eddowes' clothing or was making a wild claim concerning its authenticity. It seems certain that information appertaining to victims' clothing descriptions would be known to only a few (such as the police-officers on the scene of the crime) so there is a fair chance that it is the real thing.

I make no false claims about the shawl's authenticity, and leave that to those who feel sufficiently curious to have it forensically examined and tested. In reality, the locating of the shawl was an added bonus for my efforts over the years. It certainly proves that, although the case is over one hundred years old, it is still possible to locate and unearth new evidence, albeit rather controversial and unconnected with the direct evidence of the case. Undoubtedly, the shawl will cause much controversy among those who learn of its existence, yet I feel confident that its history is eventful and may merit further research.

Leaving the shawl behind, I will turn to what I describe as possibly the most mystifying encounter in my life in which the cynicism which has been born of my encounters with life as a police-officer proved to be inconvenient, as a more naïve individual might have profited further from the encounter. Being fortunate enough to be in a position which allows me day-to-day contact with police investigations, I have naturally accumulated a telephone directory full of contacts from all over the world, many of whom are themselves serving police-officers of all ranks. Any information required is only a phone call or letter away. None of this information is, of course, of a restricted nature, it is easily accessible once one knows what to ask for and to whom. On commencing research into this work, I made it common knowledge throughout my sphere of police contacts, that I would like to hear of any information deemed of interest. The response was excellent resulting in hundreds of telephone numbers and addresses to contact. I was amazed to find just how many policemen are keen historians of crime and social problems, and even further surprised at how many were interested in Jack the Ripper. From the information received, I had the mountainous task of collating valid evidence and possible contacts. These were religiously recorded in a notebook and stored until such time as I needed to consult someone or research something new. It was not until November 1988 that I consulted the notes and found an odd message I had left myself which read 'Barnett, possibility of existence of present day descendants'.

One of the more serious problems encountered during research was the lack of information about particular individuals, especially such a man as Joseph Barnett who was a nobody, an average everyday person whose movements were not meticulously recorded. I resolved to try and trace any known relatives, but continually drew blanks with my enquiries. Eventually, as a last resort, I telephoned dozens of persons with his surname; naturally, not once was I offered a glimmer of hope, the response was abysmal and my resilience was tested, but I refused to terminate my enquiries, so once again I scanned the names in the telephone directories. This time I wrote to the addresses of over fifty different Barnetts. For many weeks I heard nothing until one night when I was privileged to take part in a mysterious telephone conversation. The voice on the other end of the phone sounded rather unsteady, but sincere, the caller informed me that he was the man I was searching for, and that he had information which would prove beneficial to my research since Joseph Barnett had been his blood relative. I asked two searching questions about Barnett's date and place of death and received two accurate and detailed answers. I was sceptical about the whole affair, and reasoned that this fellow might also be a Ripperologist who had stumbled across information relating to Barnett. I asked if I could meet the caller and an appointment was made for a rendezvous in the Blind Beggar public house in Whitechapel Road. Without further notice the caller hung up, and I felt overwhelmed by the suspicion that someone was attempting to fool or trick me, yet I could think of no motive for such actions (though life in the police force reveals many strange incidents which transpire for no apparent reason). It was not until much later that I realized that I had not acquired the caller's number or address.

The meeting was arranged for a Saturday lunchtime, and I was asked to take a briefcase with me and to have it in full view in the pub. I was aware of the hazards of carrying a briefcase on a non-working day and attempted to keep it as inconspicuous as possible. Arriving at the pub, I sat in a plush leather chair and awaited my mysterious caller. I had just began to think about the famous murder which took place in this very same pub involving those other East End legends, the Kray twins, when I suddenly became aware of the presence of a distinguished looking gentleman who introduced himself and casually sat down on the opposite side of the table. The man, I would estimate, was aged around 70 years, and was very definitely an East-ender with a heavy London accent. Almost immediately he began questioning the purpose of my enquiries; unconvincingly, I explained why, though I failed to tell him of the evidence I had gathered through research, and gave false reasons. I was frightened of stating my suspicions too soon and in doing so frightening my contact away. I decided to apply police investigation techniques since it is much better to acquire the confidence of the interviewee before putting to him the questions which you want answered. It took almost half an hour before I was able to force home my investigative training and technique, and take the upper hand in the questioning. Asking him just why he believed his relative was the killer, I was informed that his own father believed Joseph was the Ripper as Joseph had regularly discussed the matter within the family confines and told his father that the Ripper was a local man who killed for a purpose rather than desire. He added that Joseph seemed emotional when speaking of the crimes, and would often say that he felt pity for the killer since he could not reveal his identity for fear of execution.

Continuing, I was told how Barnett had left London and moved for a short time to Leicester, a fact of which I was already aware, but nevertheless appreciated. He was friendly with another local man by the name of 'Flosser', who was hanged for his part in a serious robbery. Much of what was being said was of no value, and was the kind of data which reveals little or nothing about the individual concerned. One point upon which I did seize was the fact that he believed Joseph had undertaken patrol duties of Whitechapel/Spitalfields with the men of the Vigilance Committee. (I had already been advised by a member of Scotland Yard that Barnett was one of 'Lusk's Men'.) If this is correct, then Barnett would have found it all too easy to allay suspicion of himself as he eagerly patrolled the streets. It would also have provided Barnett with a pair of rubber-soled shoes, purportedly part of the Ripper's necessary equipment, and coincides with the description provided by Detective Stephen White who saw a man in Barnett's image leaving Mitre Square complete with rubber-soled shoes.

I asked why he had chosen to remain silent for all these years, and suggested that he could have sold his story to the press for a substantial sum. I was rebuked for this, but my partner began to display signs of uneasiness even while he provided reasonable solutions to my queries. He said that it was of no personal advantage for him to reveal his story and opinions since he was financially secure and did not want the publicity and the hassle which would inevitably follow such an announcement. He added that he felt he could not handle the ridicule which would be displayed by friends who would make light of the facts. I had never pondered over the personal opinions of someone who preferred to remain silent over the years, but I was now forced to agree that this was a logical explanation. Forcing the situation further, I threw caution to the wind, and asked for anything which could be provided which would link Barnett with the crimes. I was handed a large manilla envelope and told to be careful with the contents. As I reached inside the envelope, he said, 'That is all that remains of the life of Jack the Ripper.' Inside I found thirty-three individual newspaper cuttings dating from August 1888 right through to April 1891, all related to the Ripper murders. I could not see why they were proof of Joseph Barnett's guilt. It was then explained to me that Barnett himself had collected these cuttings. How had he known to collect the cutting referring to the Martha Tabram/Turner murder since no one then knew that a series of murders was to take place. Joseph Barnett has only been claimed to be linked with the last murder, that of Mary Kelly. The cuttings convinced me that Barnett was guilty, and also that I was speaking with a living relative of his; it seemed quite incredible that I was holding the newspaper cuttings from which Barnett had possibly read to Mary Kelly.

After almost two hours, the conversation began to falter, both of us were tired and my encounter was almost over. I explained that I needed to know my mysterious stranger's address as, when I published the story, there would be others who would wish to research it further, and might wish to speak with him. I also told him that it would prove the authenticity of the tale. Sadly, Mr Barnett declined saying that he was not at liberty to discuss his private life with anyone and refused to be used as a pawn by less honest researchers. He informed me that my research was as accurate as it could be, and that I was not to worry, I would be proved correct. Refusing to concede the point, I attempted to force the information from him, but I had met my match. Mr Barnett rose to his feet and offered his hand in a farewell gesture, then, without further ado, he was gone, returning to a life of obscurity and hopefully a peaceful existence.

The return journey to my home was non-eventful. My mind was in turmoil, how could I meet a complete stranger and believe that he would tell me personal family secrets which were interwoven with one of the greatest criminal mysteries of mankind? The problem was that I did believe the man, not because I wanted to, but for other reasons amounting to character assessment. In my opinion the man was genuine. Never once had he asked for anything in response to the information supplied, and he made no profit from any part of the encounter. From a professional point of view, I found it difficult to accept the encounter as genuine, yet something within told me otherwise. Eventually, I reasoned that it was not for me to cast aspersions on anyone's character, nor had I a divine right to interfere with the man's life. I have since tried to locate Mr Barnett, but without success. Naturally, the cynics will claim this whole scenario is fictional, but I care little for their opinions for I know that it did take place and that is all that matters. I am man enough to stand up and be counted. If one day someone comes forward and tells me it was a hoax, then I shall accept that for what it is, but it would have been a somewhat elaborate hoax for no purpose.

There you have it, nothing spectacular I admit, but

nevertheless intriguing. Having disproved every previous theory produced and provided vital evidence against Joseph Barnett, as well as an interview with a man who may be his living relative and informed me of a family belief that Joseph was the Ripper, the case is more or less complete. It is irrefutable that the chase is now over. Fellow police-officers of all ranks agree with my conclusions, theirs are professional opinions based upon years of practical policing, such officers are not easily convinced yet in this instance they are united in their opinion that Joseph Barnett was Jack the Ripper.

7 As it is Now

The East End of London which Joseph Barnett knew, has altered beyond all recognition since the time when he walked its narrow dirty streets. One hundred years have lapsed since the crimes, but there are still a few streets and buildings which he would recognize if he were to return. Many of the old derelict houses are shells, dangerous and awaiting demolition.

It is still possible to walk around the Ripper's streets and to visit the various murder sites, or what remains of them. These selfsame sites are visited by thousands of people each year, many are amateur criminologists, others are tourists reliving part of London's history. For the stranger to the district, the very thought of walking around London's meanest streets in the heart of gangland where gangsters and ruffians hang around every doorway and street corner may seem like a nightmare.

I can honestly say that, during my untold number of visits to the district in the course of research on this book, I have never encountered or witnessed any kind of trouble. In fact, I have found the people who live and dwell in this area particularly friendly. This chapter then, is for those who may never have visited the district before. It is a walking tour of the Ripper's streets.

For the uninitiated, the easiest and most direct route into the East End is to use the London underground railway taking the Metropolitan or District lines which run direct to Whitechapel. It is not a difficult place to find using a car, but I will assume most people will travel by tube.

It is apparent when travelling on London's underground just how few people actually travel to Whitechapel itself, each station along the route provides a suitable point of exit for the travelling army of shoppers and tourists. In contrast, many of those who depart at Whitechapel are about to embark on a similar adventure to you, searching the Ripper's streets, examining murder sites and their surrounding buildings, and wondering if Jack ever hid in their doorways or walked along the same cobbled streets as you.

On arrival at Whitechapel station, we depart from the tube and cross the old wooden railway bridge, which is enclosed with dirty windows and decaying wood and metal – in an attempt to disguise this it has been painted brown and cream. As we cross the bridge, we enter the station building itself which has changed very little since the Victorian era. As we step out of the station on to the massive Whitechapel Road, the first sight to meet our eyes is the huge London Hospital, built in 1866 and 1876 to house over one thousand patients, making it at the time the world's largest hospital. In present times, it remains one of the largest employers in the district; back in Victorian times, almost everyone who had a relative living in the East End also had a relative or friend who worked in some capacity at this hospital. For our purposes, the hospital is renowned for different reasons; the press of the Victorian era intimated that the Ripper was a doctor who worked at this hospital. We have not been in the area for two minutes and already we have found our first link with Jack the Ripper.

It may come as an even greater surprise to hear that as you stand on the pavement outside the station you are standing beside an important building in the Ripper investigation.

The building situated on the left side of the station as you face London Hospital, was at one time known as the Whitechapel Working Lads Institute. It is now used for a different purpose, but it is interesting to note its existence, as it has not altered its external appearance in over one hundred years. It was within this building that Coroner Wynne E. Baxter reprimanded the police for their lack of evidence during the inquests into the deaths of Polly Nichols and Annie Chapman.

Depending upon what time of day it is, you may see dozens of market stalls lining the pavements on the north side of Whitechapel Road. The stalls, made of tubular steel and plastic sheeting, are the only things which are characteristically different from the market stalls which stood on this same site one hundred years ago. On odd occasions it is possible to see an original coster's barrow with its heavy wooden frame and metal-rimmed wheels, those which can be seen are in first class condition. It seems that, apart from technological advances, very little has altered in one hundred years.

Turning left out of the station, and walking along the northern pavements of Whitechapel Road, we continue until we come to Brady Street, the first street on the left. Turning left up Brady Street, we see piles of rotting rubbish and food line the gutters, which maintain a high number of vermin. Continuing along the street we take the second turning on our left. The Roebuck public house stands on the corner. At first sight, this appears to be a narrow little street with nothing standing. The sign above the pub declares that this is Durward Street. In fact, this street was once known as Bucks Row, the scene of Joseph Barnett's first murder. Many years ago, the local residents petitioned to have its name changed from Bucks Row mainly because of its ill-found notoriety.

Looking along the street, it is hardly conceivable that it was once a narrow cobbled street surmounted by tiny terraced houses on its south side, and warehouses and slaughterhouses on its north side. The row of terraced houses is long gone, and has been replaced by a scrapyard which is hidden behind yards of corrugated tin sheeting. The warehouses which once stood on its northern side have also gone, all that remains now is a crumbling wall behind which the demolished warehouses have been flattened and packed solidly into the earth, raising its level by about four feet. Continuing along Durward Street, we arrive at an old building which stands empty and bare on the north side of the street, rotting wooden timbers stand proud like fingers reaching into the sky, once they supported the roof of this proud old building. This is the shell of Essex Wharf. If we look closely at the exposed side of the building its name can be seen built into the brickwork. Immediately opposite Essex Wharf on the south side of the street is the remains of a small entrance which is now blocked by a sheet of corrugated metal. In this entrance, Polly Nichols breathed her last. The most striking feature to note is how near the front door and window of Essex Wharf are to the murder site. Immediately above the front door of the wharf is the bedroom window where Mrs Walter Purkess lay awake all night, while her husband occasionally peered out of the window. It seems impossible to believe that a murder was committed right outside this window without any sound being heard.

Standing next to the murder site, is the giant shell of the board school, once a very impressive building it now stands empty, ravaged by the elements and time, its doorways blocked up with modern breeze blocks. Every time I see this building I wonder what secrets it could reveal if it could talk. Its windows have long gone, and the darkness behind the frames conjures up all sorts of images. High on its roof stands a row of unhealthy looking railings, these in fact marked the outer extremities of the school playground and prevented unnecessary deaths. The reason it was so situated was because of the lack of space on the ground. During the hours of darkness, Durward Street takes on a different appearance, the shells of Essex Wharf and the board school come alive, and one can imagine Polly Nichols staggering along the road to her death. The street is still very badly illuminated, and the whole area will probably disappear in a few years. Apart from the people drinking in the Roebuck public house, the only others to pass along the street after dark are Ripperologists or vagrants looking for somewhere to sleep. Graffiti covers the area, and one comment chalked on to the wall next to the murder site declares, 'Jacks Back'.

Walking past the board school, the thoroughfare opens out into one broad street without any real buildings. The street ends at Vallance Road which was famous for being the street where the Kray twins lived at 'Fort Vallance'. One hundred years ago it was known as Bakers Row, but since those days it has been greatly altered, mainly due to the effects of wartime bombing raids. Turning right along Vallance Road, then almost immediately left, we follow Old Montague Street. We have now walked the route taken by carman Cross when he went in search of a policeman after finding the body of Polly Nichols in Bucks Row. This is also the route taken by the police when they wheeled the body of Nichols to the mortuary. Old Montague Street bears no resemblance to its appearance in Victorian days, all of the houses have been replaced by modern flats and office blocks, only the street name remains intact. At the end of Old Montague Street we come to the junction of Osborn Street and Brick Lane. Turn right along Brick Lane, a street which derives its name from the fourteenth-century brickworks and brickfields which supplied the majority of London with building materials. Brick Lane is a long narrow street, deep in the heart of Ripper country. Joseph Barnett once resided with Mary Kelly in this street, the house where they lived has gone, but the pubs are still standing. As we continue along Brick Lane we pass streets which have become synonymous with Jack the Ripper: Thrawl Street, Flower and Dean Street (which has now altered drastically), Fashion Street, Fournier Street ... these streets once contained thousands of homeless people many of whom would sleep on the tiny pavements or anywhere they could find that was free from any kind of excrement. Today, the majority of these streets are filled with warehouses, the doss-houses have been knocked into giant factory premises, all that remains are the doorways, bricked up many years ago.

Six blocks from Osborn Street along Brick Lane we come to the crossing with Hanbury Street. Turning left into Hanbury Street, it becomes apparent that one side has been demolished to make way for a giant brewery complex. More disconcerting is the fact that the side of the street which has been demolished is the one where number 29 once stood. The opposite side of the street has hardly altered from 1888, but the atmosphere has gone; however, a close inspection of the properties in surrounding streets reveals that similar-style passages and rear yards still exist. The thing that immediately meets you as you walk along the passages of such houses is the damp smell of rotting wood; as you walk through the house along the passage and step out into the rear yard, it is like stepping into a different world, the dimensions and layout of some of the yards are almost exactly the same as 29 Hanbury Street would have been. Continuing along Hanbury Street, which is not a long road, we emerge on to Commercial Street, a busy road and easily recognizable by the volume of traffic. Standing on the far side of the road is the gigantic green Spitalfields market, once the largest of its kind in the world.

Turn left into Commercial Street and continue along past the Ten Bells public house on the corner of Fournier Street, once known as Church Street. The pub was once called the Jack the Ripper, but had to revert to its original title for political reasons. The pub itself is well worth a visit, its walls are plastered with Ripper literature and, after all, once you have taken a drink within this public house you can claim to have drunk in the same pub as Jack the Ripper. The Ten Bells was by far and away the most popular pub during the Ripper's reign of terror, Joseph Barnett used it, as did Mary Kelly and all the other victims.

Standing almost on the doorstep of the pub is the famous church of Christchurch Spitalfields, a magnificent building which is out of keeping with the rest of the area. Adjoining the church are some small gardens, officially titled Christchurch Gardens, but known locally as 'Itchy Park' after the hundreds of vagrants who used the area as a meeting place, most of whom were infested with lice and other such creatures making everyone who passed through the gardens itch. Almost opposite 'Itchy Park', on the other side of Commercial Street, stands an ultra-modern multi-storey car-park, which is a definite eyesore. Running between the car-park and some offices is a tiny private road. There is nothing extraordinary about the road, it is used as access to the offices and for spare car-parking places and is called Duval Street. It was once Dorset Street! One's first impression is just how small the street is, it can hardly be two hundred yards long. Approximately thirty-five paces in from Commercial Street, on the right-hand side of Duval Street stands an archway, this is the approximate site of the entrance to Millers Court. One of my first visits to the area resulted in my immense disappointment when I discovered that Millers Court was no more. Close examination of the tarmac road reveals that great lumps have lifted, exposing the original cobbled brick road which was once Dorset Street. It is impossible to believe that Duval Street was once classed as the roughest street in London, if not the world, today it is possibly the cleanest street in the district. Just how all those people managed to live in this one tiny street is beyond me. At night, Duval Street is transformed into an eerie passage, a chill runs up my spine every time I walk its length. I have been sure of another's presence there on a number of occasions, but I have never turned around to look!

The streets surrounding Duval Street are very well preserved; in some alleys, there is hardly sufficient room for two people to pass, and the area is full of atmosphere. At the far end of Duval Street lies Crispin Street with its old style shops which must have been used by Barnett and Kelly. Many of the buildings in Crispin Street date from the nineteenth century. Also in Crispin Street is a women's refuge, the nuns who live there believe that Mary Kelly was once brought up in this refuge and trained as a housemaid. Unfortunately it is only a myth, and there is no documentary evidence to support this.

Turn left down Crispin Street, this leads us into Bell Lane, and the street ends at the Wentworth Street crossroads. Cross straight over the crossroads and into Goulston Street. From the corner of the crossroads, one third of the way down the east side of Goulston Street stands an empty building, this is Wentworth Dwellings, or at least part of the original buildings. Each one of the doorways to this building has been blocked off. It was in a similar entrance that the legendary 'Juwes' message was scrawled and a piece of Catharine Eddowes' apron was found. That particular doorway and building were knocked down some years ago, but similar entrances can still be found. The doorways are quite distinctive in appearance, they are surmounted by an ornamental latticework in white plaster of a ball and circle design. The remaining building is a long overdue candidate for demolition, and I believe it will only be a short time before another piece of Victorian architecture disappears from our skyline.

Our next port of call is Mitre Square. For the stranger to the district, this is not the easiest place to find, although with local knowledge it is possible to make the journey in a few minutes. However, we will stick to the primary routes. Continuing along Goulston Street eventually leads us back on to Whitechapel High Street, once here we make a right turn. Follow the road down into Aldgate, the traffic and pavement areas are much busier here, but a subway system for pedestrians alleviates major problems. Four blocks down from Goulston Street on the northern side of the street, we arrive at Mitre Street. Hidden behind a large school is tiny Mitre Square. Walking along Mitre Street, we can remember how Constable Edward Watkins walked this very same beat in the early hours of 30 September 1888. Turn right into Mitre Square, on the right-hand side is a set of gates giving access to the rear of the school. It was in this corner of the square that Catharine Eddowes was dispatched to her Maker on that fateful night. The cobbled stones of the square still exist and the actual dimensions of the cobbled area have not changed since 1888. This is a very quiet secluded area, which is surprising when you consider that busy Aldgate is only just behind the buildings surrounding the square.

Once again, in the hours of darkness, Mitre Square is transformed, anyone who passes through the square does so rather quickly, preferring not to stop and think about what took place here one hundred years ago. There is talk of the square being haunted, and I know of a dozen people who have witnessed strange sights in the corner where Catharine Eddowes' body was found, I personally cannot deny or confirm any such visions, but it is not difficult to imagine such occurrences. I have a closer affinity with Mitre Square than any of the other murder sites, mainly because the first time I visited it, I felt quite inconsequential within its surroundings and could practically imagine Jack the Ripper walking away from the body of Eddowes across the cobbled stones. The square is still quite small, but it has been opened out since 1888, not one of the buildings which surrounded the dimensions of the square remains they have all been replaced by modern office blocks and this spoils the illusion.

On the northern side of the square a plaque is mounted into a wall. It has the appearance of blue marble and reads 'Site of the Priory of the Holy Trinity founded 1108'. The Holy Trinity was founded by Matilda, wife of Henry I, as a house for Augustinian canons. It was sometimes called Christchurch priory, sometimes 'Holy Trinity'. The priory comprised several old parishes – St Mary Magdalene, St Michael, St Katherine and the Blessed Trinity – all were united under the name of the Holy Cross or Holy Rood parish and after the foundations of the priory it was formed into the parish of the Holy Trinity. The bull of Pope Innocent in 1137 confirming the foundation mentions the church of St Katherine and the chapel of St Michael in the churchyard of the monastery.

There is a legend concerning two canons of the Holy Trinity Priory who were having an argument of no consequence, when one drew a dagger and mortally wounded his fellow. He then mutilated his own person before plunging the dagger into his heart, this was presumably done to give the act the appearance of self-defence.

The priory was dissolved in 1531 and the site granted to Sir Thomas Audley, who pulled it down selling the stone to make paving. Audley erected a house on the site, which was later called Dukes Place, and so the history of Mitre Square was formed.

Leaving the square by the way we entered, we return along Whitechapel High Street and come to a very busy junction in the road. Here we take a right turn off the High Street down on to Commercial Road. This manœuvre is made less difficult by efficient use of the labyrinth of subway tunnels and we eventually surface on Commercial Road. By now, the keen Ripperologist will have realized that the mean streets of Jack the Ripper are no different to that of any other town, the Victoriana is all but gone, and has made way for the new city. It is a major disappointment, but life goes on, and one could not expect the borough councils to maintain the murder sites. At least we can visit them without too much trouble, though future generations will encounter a great deal more in the way of problems when they come to visit this same area. It seems that each time I return to Whitechapel/Spitalfields, another building or landmark has disappeared to make way for a supermarket or a car-park.

Five blocks along Commercial Road on its south side is Henriques Street, beneath its street sign is a clue as to our destination, for another sign states 'Formerly Berner Street'. The street is no longer than one hundred yards, but it bears no resemblance to how it appeared in 1888. On the right-hand side of the street stands an old school, ironically, the school was built to replace the slums of the Victorian era. It was in one of these slums that the tiny Dutfields Yard stood (Number 40). Again there is a feeling of disappointment, as not the slightest piece of Victoriana exists, we can only imagine what it must have been like. The school playground cannot be entered without permission, but I see no real purpose in looking at a piece of open ground because it was the murder site of Elizabeth Stride. The air is filled by the shouts and screams of young children enjoying themselves, yet on this very site, one of the most legendary crimes in criminal history took place. This is ironic justice.

So the Ripper walk is completed, each of the five murder sites has been visited.

For the keener student the walk need not end here since other venues can be visited. Some are of no real importance, but are well worth a visit. Pinchin Street, for example, where the torso of a woman was found under a railway arch, has not changed at all and the arch still stands. Swallow Gardens (Chamber Street) where the body of Frances Coles was found, is situated south of Berner Street (Henriques Street).

George Yard Buildings stands at the bottom end of Gunthorpe Street, a narrow alley leading off Whitechapel High Street. The murder site is untouched by time, but unfortunately it is in an inaccessible position at the rear of a well-to-do restaurant, and the management would not appreciate dozens of Ripperologists tramping through his premises. For information the restaurant is called Bloom's.

During the research for this book I spent many hours talking to local residents, and heard many tales, some of Jack the Ripper and some of the local environment. I was informed by more than one person that Gunthorpe Street, once George Yard, was known locally as 'Shit Alley'. This was because of the high percentage of stableyards situated in the narrow sloping cobbled streets. The gutters were lined with both human and animal excreta, and when it rained, this flowed down the gutters creating the most awful stench imaginable. Not a pleasant tale I admit, but one which truly epitomizes life in Whitechapel during the Victorian era.

Please remember, when you are tramping around this district, that occasionally you may be encroaching on someone else's property. It is a good idea to ask anyone working in a building or yard if you can have a look around. This also means that you may hear some good tales while carrying out your tour. Almost all of the pubs are worth a visit, with the Frying Pan and the Ten Bells being the most popular.

The Victims

Mary Ann Nichols

Born 26 August 1845.
Died 31 August 1888.
Buried at the East London Cemetery, public grave number 11217.

Eliza Anne Chapman

Born 1841.
Died 8 September 1888.
Buried at the East London Cemetery, public grave number 12439.

Liz Stride

Born 27 November 1843.
Died 30 September 1888.
Buried at the East London Cemetery, public grave number 15509.

Catharine Eddowes

Born 14 April 1842.
Died 30 September 1888.
Buried at the East London Cemetery, public grave number 49336, square 318.

Mary Jane Kelly

Born 1862.
Died 9 November 1888.
Buried at St Patrick's Roman Catholic Cemetery, Leytonstone, grave 16, row 67.

Selected Bibliography

Anderson, Robert, *The Lighter Side of my Official life.* (Nisbet, 1907).

Cullen, Tom, *Autumn of Terror* (Bodley Head, 1965).

Farson, Dan, *Jack the Ripper* (Michael Joseph, 1972).

Fido, Martin, *The Crimes, Detection and Death of Jack the Ripper* (Weidenfield & Nicholson, 1987).

Harris, Melvyn, *The Bloody Truth* (Columbus Books, 1987).

Harrison, Michael, *Clarence* (W.H. Allen, 1972).

Jones, Elwyn and Lloyd, John, *The Ripper File* (Arthur Barker, 1975).

Knight, Stephen, *Jack the Ripper: The Final Solution* (George G. Harrap, 1976).

McCormick, Donald, *The Identity of Jack the Ripper* (Jarrolds, 1959).

MacNaghton, Melville, *Days of My Years* (Arnold, 1915).

Matters, Leonard, *Jack the Ripper* (Hutchinson, 1929).

Minto, G.A., *The Thin Blue Line* (Hodder & Stoughton, 1965).

Odell, Robin, *Jack the Ripper in Fact and Fiction* (George G. Harrap, 1965).

Rumbelow, Donald, *The Complete Jack the Ripper* (W.H. Allen, 1975).

Sharkey, Terence, *Jack the Ripper, One Hundred Years of Investigation,* (Ward Lock, 1987).

Shew, E. Spencer, *A Companion to Murder* (Cassell, 1960).

Silberman, Charles, *Criminal Violence, Criminal Justice* (Random House, New York, 1978).

Stephenson, Roslyn D'Onston, *The Patristic Gospels* (Grant Richards, 1904).

Smith, Major Henry, *From Constable to Commissioner, (The story of sixty years, most of them misspent)* (Chatto & Windus, 1910).

Underwood, Peter, *Jack the Ripper, One Hundred Years of Mystery* (Blandford Press, 1987).

Other Sources

MEPO Files (The Whitechapel Murders): 3/140, 3/141, 3/142.
Home Office Files (The Whitechapel Murders): A49301; 144/220, A49301..a,b,c,d,e,f,g,h,j,k.

Police Gazette, Police Review, The Lancet, The Talkthrough, The Criminologist, Police Journal, Illustrated Police News, Daily Mail, Daily Express, Reynolds News, Daily Telegraph, Pall Mall Gazette, The Sun, The Star, The People, Northampton Evening Telegraph, Cumberland Newspapers Group, *Yorkshire Evening Post, East London Advertiser, East London Telephone Directory, Exchange and Mart,* Coroners Inquest Papers Corporation of London Records Office and information passed to me verbally by hundreds of interested parties.

Index